THE CITIZENSHIP HANDBOOK

GUIA PARA LA CIUDADANIA

THE CITIZENSHIP HANDBOOK
GUIA PARA LA CIUDADANIA

Barbara E. Goldin

Spanish Version by
Flamm/Northam Authors
and Publishers Services, Inc.

MONARCH
PRESS

MONARCH PRESS and colophon are registered trademarks
of Simon & Schuster, Inc.

Designed by Irving Perkins Associates

Manufactured in the United States of America

10 9 8 7 6 5 4 3 2 1

Library of Congress Catalog Card Number: 82-63203

ISBN: O-671-45331-9

This book is dedicated
in loving honor to my paternal grandparents
Abraham Goldin and
Gertrude Solomon Goldin
and in loving memory of my maternal grandparents
Abraham Samuel Weisner and
Bertha Winkelman Weisner
Four immigrants who helped build America

Dedico este libro
en honor a mis abuelos paternos
Abraham Goldin y
Gertrude Salomon de Goldin
y en memoria de mis abuelos maternos
Abraham Samuel Weisner y
Bertha Winkelman de Weisner
cuatro inmigrantes que ayudaron a hacer
los Estados Unidos de Norteamerica

AGRADECIMIENTO

Mi más profundo reconocimiento a Siret Yenner y los otros functionarios de la biblioteca pública de Madison Heights (Michigan) por su esmerada ayuda en la preparación de este manual.

ACKNOWLEDGMENTS

Special thanks to Siret Yenner and the other staff members of the Madison Heights Public Library for their very fine assistance in the preparation of this handbook.

CONTENIDO

CONTENTS

INTRODUCCION

Amable Lector:

Si piensas inmigrar a los Estados Unidos, este libro es para ti. Si ya estás en los Estados Unidos y piensas convertirte en ciudadano, este libro te ayudará a prepararte para el examen de ciudadanía.

LA GUIA PARA LA CIUDADANÍA ESTADOUNIDENSE consta de tres partes. En la *Primera Parte*, aprenderás todo lo que tienes que saber sobre la entrada a los Estados Unidos para establecer tu residencia aquí. Ir a un país diferente al país nativo para establecerse allí permanentemente se llama "inmigración." La *Primera Parte* de este libro te enseñará sobre la inmigración a los Estados Unidos y la solicitud de la ciudadanía. Verás lo que tienes que hacer para presentar el examen de ciudadanía y dónde debes ir para presentarlo. Te enterarás también sobre cuánto tiempo te tardarás en volverte ciudadano.

Al final de la *Primera Parte* encontrarás una lista de Oficinas de Inmigración, oficinas que tiene el gobierno de los Estados Unidos para atender a los inmigrantes. Hay oficinas en todo el país. Alguna te quedará cerca. Siempre puedes acudir a estas oficinas para hacer preguntas o para buscar ayuda.

INTRODUCTION

Dear Reader:

If you are planning to immigrate to America, this book is for you. If you are already in America and are planning to become a citizen, this book will assist you in preparing for the U.S. citizenship test.

The Citizenship Handbook has three parts. In *Part One*, you will learn everything that you have to know about coming to the United States and becoming a citizen. You will find out what you need to learn to take the citizenship test, and where you should go to take it. You will also learn how long it will take for you to become a citizen.

At the end of *Part One* is a list of immigration offices around the country. One will be near you. You can always go there to ask questions or to get help.

Part Two is for people who are getting ready to become citizens. The process of becoming a citizen is called *naturalization*. To become a citizen, or to be naturalized, you have to know some facts about American government and history. To become naturalized, you must take a test to show what you have learned. *Part Two* will help you to prepare for the citizenship test. It contains the kinds of questions that you will be asked on the test. You are also

La *Segunda Parte* es para aquellas personas que planean convertirse en ciudadanos. Este proceso se llama "naturalización." Para convertirte en ciudadano, o sea para naturalizarte, tienes que saber algunos hechos de la historia de los Estados Unidos y de su sistema político. Para naturalizarte, debes presentar un examen para mostrar lo que has aprendido. La *Segunda Parte* te ayudará a prepararte para este examen de ciudadanía. Contiene el tipo de preguntas que te harán en el examen. Se te dará también las respuestas y unas explicaciones para comprender mejor las preguntas. Si lees la *Segunda Parte* con ciudado aprenderás las cosas que tienes que saber para salir bien en el examen.

En la *Tercera Parte* hay una lista de preguntas y respuestas breves. Estas son de repaso. Trata de dar la respuesta antes de leerla. Es una buena práctica antes de presentar el examen de verdad.

No intentes leer todo el libro de una vez. No esperes recordar todo. Más bien, lee un poco cada día. Si puedes, busca la ayuda de un amigo de habla inglesa, un pariente o un vecino. Si no tienes a quién recurrir, no te preocupes. De todas maneras, con este libro puedes aprender las cosas que debes saber.

Te deseo buena suerte en los Estados Unidos de Norteamerica, tu nueva patria.

Barbara E. Goldin

given answers and explanations to help you understand the questions. If you read *Part Two* carefully, you will learn the things that you have to know to do well on the test.

In *Part Three* there is another list of questions and short answers. These are for review. Try to answer these questions yourself before reading the answers. They are good practice for you before you take the real test.

Don't try to read all of this book at one time. Nor should you expect to remember everything. Instead, try to read a little bit each day. If you can, try to get an English-speaking friend, relative, or neighbor to help you. If you don't have anyone to ask, don't worry. You can still learn the things you need to know by using this book.

Good luck to you in America, your new home.

Barbara E. Goldin

PREFACIO

¡Así que te estás preparando para tu examen de ciudadanía! No estás solo; más de 210,000 inmigrantes se naturalizan como ciudadanos norteamericanos cada año. Encontrarás bastante ayuda en el proceso. La mayoría de los programas educativos para adultos en las grandes cuidades, tales como el Program "C 3," en Detroit, tienen profesores idóneos tanto de "ESL" (Inglés como Segundo Idioma) como de estudios para la ciudadanía.

Muchos aspirantes se ponen cada vez más nerviosos cuando se acerca la fecha del examen de ciudadanía. Alan Bennett, abogado de naturalización, relata la anécdota de un joven quien se puso tan nervioso que cuando el magistrado le preguntó su nombre se desmayó allí mismo. El señor Bennett nos asegura que tal temor no tiene fundamentos, pues más o menos un 90 por ciento de todos los aspirantes aprueban sus exámenes. ¡Así que tus posibilidades de aprobar son excelentes! La mayoría de los aspirantes a la ciudadanía tienen tres preocupaciones principales. Estas son: prestar el juramento de lealtad, comprobar sus conocimientos del inglés y saber lo suficiente sobre la historia y el sistema político estadounidense para aprobar el examen.

PREFACE

So you are preparing to apply for your citizenship exam! You are not alone; over 210,000 immigrants become naturalized citizens each year in the United States. You'll find quite a lot of help along the way. Most of the adult education programs in the major cities, such as Project C3 in Detroit, have well-qualified instructors of both ESL (English as a Second Language) and citizenship studies.

Many applicants find themselves growing more and more nervous as the date of their citizenship exam gets closer. Alan Bennett, a naturalization attorney, tells a story about a young man who was so nervous that, when asked by the judge what his name was, he fainted on the spot! Mr. Bennett assures us such fear is unfounded; close to 90 percent of the applicants pass their exams. As you can see, your chances for passing are excellent! Most citizenship applications worry about three things: taking the oath of allegiance, proving their proficiency in English, and knowing enough about American history and government to pass the exam.

La cuestión de jurar bandera es tal vez el dilema más difícil que enfrentan los aspirantes. Nuha Arenke, una ciudadana naturalizada de los Estados Unidos, nacida en Palestina, anteriormente Directora de Estudios del Instituto Internacional de Detroit, y hoy asesora de inmigración de alto rango, por más de 22 años ha brindado ayuda a los inmigrantes recién llegados. La señora Arenke recalca la importancia de la responsabilidad que conlleva el renunciar a la lealtad a tu país de origen. Ella cree que en verdad uno no puede desligarse totalmente de los sentimientos patrios por su país de origen y sus tradiciones culturales. Sin embargo, no debe haber duda alguna sobre el juramento de lealtad a los Estados Unidos en el caso de guerra en el territorio norteamericano. Indudablemente, la lealtad a los Estados Unidos es un compromiso muy fuerte, y muchos aspirantes no captan la importancia de esta cuestión. La señora Arenke desanima a aquéllos que hacen juramento ligeramente e insiste en que todo aspirante se haga un examen de conciencia antes de prestar el juramento de lealtad.

Además de ser un asunto serio, también es una experiencia emocionante (convertirse en ciudadano norteamericano). La plena participación en la vida estadounidense depende de la naturalización.

Además de la cuestión de lealtad, muchos aspirantes, especialmente los de avanzada edad, se preocupan por sus conocimientos del inglés. En el año 1978 se decretó que en el caso de aspirantes mayores de 50 años que lleven más de 20 años en los Estados Unidos al solicitar la ciudadanía, el requisito del inglés se puede suprimir. Si crees que esta ley es aplicable en tu caso, averigua los procedimientos en el Departamento de Inmigración y Naturalización más cercano.

Probably the most difficult issue that most applicants face is the question of allegiance. Nuha Arenke, a Palestinian-born naturalized American citizen herself, is the former director of educational studies at the International Institute of Detroit and a senior immigration counselor. She has been helping newly arrived immigrants for over twenty-two years. Mrs. Arenke emphasizes that taking an oath to renounce your allegiance to your native country is a big responsibility. She feels that, truthfully, one cannot divorce himself or herself completely from his or her feelings of allegiance to his or her home country and ethnic background. However, there should be no question of allegiance to the United States if a war were ever fought on American soil. There is no doubt that American allegiance is a matter of strong commitment, and many applicants do not understand the weight of the problem. Mrs. Arenke discourages those who would take the oath lightly and strongly recommends that a person really examine his or her conscience before taking it.

Although it is serious business, becoming an American citizen is a thrilling experience as well. Only after being naturalized can a person fully participate in American life.

Besides the question of allegiance, many applicants, especially older ones, worry about their competency in English. In 1978, a new ruling was passed which states that if an applicant is over fifty years old and has been here for over twenty years when he or she files for citizenship, the English requirement may be waived. If you think that this law may apply for you, check with your local Department of Immigration and Naturalization for details.

De todas maneras, es reconfortante saber que se dan clases de inglés, o sea ESL (pronúnciese: i-es-el) en todo el país y que seguramente hay una clase cercana a ti. Si llamas por teléfono a la Junta Educativa local algún funcionario te informará sobre el sitio más conveniente para tomar las clases.

No olvides que el dominio del inglés no se logra con sólo tomar clases sino con la práctica diaria también. Hay muchos libros buenos de "inglés fácil," además de un periódico llamado *News For You*, destinados especialmente para tu uso. Ver televisión, charlar con un vecino o ir de compras pueden ser ocasiones para practicar el inglés. Si asistes a las clases y practicas el inglés con regularidad, no tendrás ningún problema al solicitar la ciudadanía.

El último de los tres problemas que he mencionado en relación a las preocupaciones de los aspirantes es el de su conocimiento de la historia y sistema político de los Estados Unidos.

El señor Bennett explica que generalmente el examen consiste en siete u ocho preguntas sobre estos temas. Puede ser un examen subjetivo puesto que cada examinador decide cuáles preguntas debe hacer. Sin embargo, hay muchos conocimientos básicos que te capacitarán para aprobar el examen. Enseñarte estos conocimientos es el propósito de esta *Guía para la Ciudadanía*. El libro fue diseñado para ti. El contenido consta de los hechos que debes saber para el examen. Barbara Goldin escribió el libro basándose en su experiencia personal en los nueve años que lleva en la enseñanza tanto de inglés como de estudios para la ciudadanía con aspirantes como tú.

El formato de este manual se presta para el repaso inmediato después de cada parte. Las preguntas están formuladas para permitir al que usa el manual recordar fácilmente la información.

It is comforting to know, though, that ESL classes are being taught virtually everywhere across the country and that there is certainly one close to you. If you call your local school system, someone will direct you to the most convenient location.

Don't forget that English competency comes not only with classroom learning but also with daily practice. There are many fine "easy English" books as well as a newspaper, *News For You*, that are designed especially for your use. Even watching television, talking with a neighbor, or taking a shopping trip can be a way to exercise your English. By regularly attending classes and making use of your English, you should have no language problems by the time you file for citizenship.

The last problem I mentioned that applicants worry about is their knowledge of American history and government. Mr. Bennett explains that the average citizenship exam consists of probably seven or eight questions concerning this area. It can be a subjective test, because each examiner decides which questions he will ask. However, there is a lot of basic knowledge that will enable you to pass the exam. Teaching you that knowledge is the purpose of *The Citizenship Handbook*. This book was designed with you in mind. The contents of the book are facts that you will need to know for the exam. Barbara Goldin has written the handbook from her own nine years of personal experience in teaching both ESL and citizenship to applicants such as yourself.

The format of this handbook enables one to have immediate recall after each unit. The questions are designed to allow anyone using the handbook to easily remember the information.

La autora ha escrito el manual en el mismo orden que uno necesita la información para preparar el examen de ciudadanía.

Estoy segura que tu camino a la ciudadanía será un poco más fácil gracias a este libro.

Roberta Pittman
Directora del Programa C 3
Educación Básica para Adultos

Escuelas Públicas de Detroit
Detroit, Michigan

The author has purposefully written the handbook to flow in the same manner as one needs the information, in order to prepare for the citizenship test.

I am sure that your road to citizenship will be a little easier to travel, thanks to this book.

Roberta Pittman
Project C3 Director
Adult Basic Education

Detroit Public Schools
Detroit, Michigan

Part One
NATURALIZATION INFORMATION

Primera Parte
INFORMACION SOBRE LA NATURALIZACION

ESTA parte del libro es para aquella personas que piensan inmigrar a los Estados Unidos. No debes sentirte solo. Aproximadamente 500,000 personas inmigran a este país cada año.

En las páginas siguientes, encontrarás toda la información necesaria para comenzar el proceso de inmigración hasta conseguir la "tarjeta verde," el documento que necesitas para trabajar en los Estados Unidos.

THIS part of the book is for people who are thinking about immigrating to the United States. You aren't alone. Approximately five hundred thousand people immigrate to this country every year.

On the pages that follow, you will find all the information you need to start the immigration process right through to getting a green card, the document you need to work in the United States.

1
La Inmigración en los Estados Unidos

Para poder inmigrar a los Estados Unidos, necesitas un *patrocinador*, un padrino. A veces lo llaman también un *peticionario*. El patrocinador es alguien que vive en los Estados Unidos y asume la responsabilidad por ti hasta que tú lo puedes hacer por tu cuenta. Esta persona debe estar dispuesta a mantenerte y ayudarte.

Un patrocinador es, por lo general, un pariente, como un padre o un hermano. A veces él es un patrón. Tú eres *el beneficiario*, o sea la persona que se beneficia con la ayuda del patrocinador.

Los Trámites de Inmigración

El primer paso de todos lo da el patrocinador. Debe ir a una Oficina de Inmigración a pedir bien sea el Formulario I-130. Debe llenar la solicitud y devolverla, adjuntando diez dólares americanos (US$10.00), a la Oficina de Inmigración.

1
Immigrating to the United States

In order to immigrate to the United States, you need a *sponsor*. A sponsor is also called a *petitioner*. He or she is someone who is already living in the United States. This person accepts the responsibility for taking care of you until you can do so yourself. He or she has to be willing to support and help you.

A sponsor is usually a close relative such as a parent, a brother, or a sister. Sometimes he or she is an employer. You are the *beneficiary*, or the person who receives help from the sponsor.

Immigration Proceedings

The first step is for the sponsor to go to the Immigration Office and ask for Form I-130. The sponsor fills out the application and returns it, with ten dollars ($10), to the Immigration Office.

Cuando la solicitud esté en regla, la Oficina de Inmigración la remitirá al Consulado Norteamericano en tu país. Después de repasar la solicitud, el Consulado te citará para solicitar la visa. La visa es tu permiso escrito para entrar en los Estados Unidos.

Cuando vayas al Consulado para conseguir la visa, debes llevar tres (3) cosas. Primero, traes tu *partida de nacimiento*, o alguna otra prueba de cuándo y dónde naciste. Segundo, traes una *carta de la policía*. Esta carta demuestra que no eres un criminal y que eres persona de buen carácter. Esta carta es un certificado de buena conducta. Tercero, traes tu *pasaporte*.

Una vez en el consulado, te indicarán que llenes una solicitud. Esta solicitud es el Formulario OF-230.

El paso siguiente consiste en ir al médico para un examen físico. El propósito principal para el examen físico es el de averiguar si tienes alguna enfermedad contagiosa.

Después del examen médico tendrás que esperar unos seis meses. A veces se necesita más tiempo y a veces se demora menos. Después de este lapso de espera, te darán la visa de inmigración. Ahora te puedes trasladar a los Estados Unidos.

Después de estar en los Estados Unidos por un tiempo de seis meses a un año, conseguirás la tarjeta verde. Una tarjeta verde significa que puedes permanecer libremente en los Estados Unidos por el tiempo que quieras. Ahora puedes comenzar a trabajar.

When the application is in order, the Immigration Office will send it to the American consulate in your country. After the application has been reviewed by the consulate, you will be notified.

When you go to the consulate to get a visa, you should bring three (3) things. First, bring a *birth certificate*, or some proof of when you were born. Second, bring a *letter from the police*. This letter shows that you are not a troublemaker and that you are a person of good character. This letter is called police clearance. Third, bring your *passport*.

At the consulate, you will be asked to fill out an application. This application is called Form OF-230.

The next step is to go to a doctor for a physical examination. The main reason for the physical examination is to check that you don't have a contagious illness.

After the physical, you will have to wait about six months. Sometimes more time is needed and sometimes less time passes. After this waiting period, you will be given an immigration visa. An immigration visa is your written permission to enter the United States. Now you are free to move to the United States.

After you have been in America for six months to a year, you will get a *green card*. This is a permanent residence card. A green card means that you are welcome to stay in the United States for as long as you want to. Now you can start working.

2
La Solicitud de Naturalización

En los Estados Unidos existen algunos requisitos, o sea leyes, referentes a la naturalización. Para poder ser aspirante a la ciudadanía debes haber cumplido 18 años de edad como mínimo. Debes ser persona de buen carácter. Debes tener la tarjeta verde. Debes llevar un mínimo de cinco (5) años en los Estados Unidos. Sin embargo, si estás casado con una persona de ciudadanía estadounidense sólo debes llevar un mínimo de tres (3) años antes de poder naturalizarte. Por último, debes saber hablar, leer y escribir algo de inglés. Tienes que demostrar que comprendes este idioma. También debes saber un poco sobre la historia y el sistema político de los Estados Unidos. Lo que debes saber más específicamente se encuentra en la Segunda Parte de este libro.

Haciendo la Solicitud

Cuando estés listo para hacer la solicitud de la ciudadanía, debes seguir estos pasos a continuación. Primero, comunícate con la Oficina de Inmigración más cercana. Hay una

2
Filing for Naturalization

The United States has some requirements, or laws, for being naturalized. To be an applicant for citizenship, you must be at least 18 years old. You must be a person of good character. You must have a green card. You must have been in the United States for at least five (5) years. Or, if you are married to an American citizen, then you only have to live here for three (3) years before you can be naturalized. Finally, you should know how to speak, read, and write some English. You must show you understand the language. You should also know a little about American history and government. What you need to know more specifically is discussed in Part Two of this book.

Filing

When you are ready to file for citizenship, here are the steps you should follow. First, contact the Immigration Office closest to your home. There is a list of Immigration Offices

lista de estas oficinas en este capítulo. Tienes que conseguir el formulario para la naturalización en una Oficina de Inmigración. Es el Formulario N-400. Es extenso y tal vez será necesario que alguien te ayude a llenarlo.

Antes de devolver el formulario, tienes que hacer dos cosas más. Primero, tienes que conseguir tus *huellas digitales*. Si llevas el formulario a la jefatura de policía local, allá te pueden tomar las huellas digitales. Estas se usan para asegurar que no seas un criminal. Son también una clase de certificado de buena conducta. Luego, necesitas *tres (3) fotografías pequeñas tuyas*. Después de conseguir las huellas digitales y las fotos, mándalas por correo con el Formulario N-400 ya completado a la Oficina de Inmigración. Esta vez tendrás que esperar por un período de seis meses a un año y medio. Cuando se haya tramitado completamente tu solicitud, recibirás una carta de la Oficina de Inmigración citándote para la Naturalización. Ahora debes empezar a prepararte para el examen de ciudadanía.

Presentando el Examen

Para presentar el examen tienes que saber algo sobre la historia y el sistema político de los Estados Unidos. Tienes que demostrar que sabes leer, escribir y hablar inglés.

Los Pasos Finales

En la fecha para el examen y tu naturalización tienes que pagar veinticinco dólares (US$25.00), para cubrir los gastos.

Después de presentar el examen de ciudadanía, estás listo a naturalizarte. Te presentas ante un magistrado quien dirá

later in this chapter. You must get a citizenship application from them. This application is Form N-400. It is a long form, and you may need help filling it out.

Before you send back the completed form, you need to do two other things. First, you need to get a set of your *fingerprints*. If you take the form to your local police station, they will make a set of fingerprints for you. The fingerprints are used to check to make sure you are not a criminal. They are also a type of police clearance. Then, you need *three (3) small photographs* of yourself. After you have gathered a set of fingerprints, and three pictures of yourself, mail them back, along with the completed Form N-400 to the Immigration Office. This time, you will have to wait six months to one and a half years. When your application has been processed, or completed, you will receive a letter from the Immigration Office telling you when to come for naturalization. At this time you should start getting ready to take the citizenship test.

Taking the Test

To take the citizenship test, you must know something about U.S. history and government. You must demonstrate your ability to read, write, and speak English.

The Final Steps

On the date that you go to take your test and become naturalized, you must pay a fee of twenty-five dollars ($25).

After you pass your citizenship exam, you are ready to be naturalized. You go before a judge who will say the oath of allegiance slowly and ask you to repeat it after him or her.

lentamente el juramento de lealtad a los Estados Unidos y tú lo repetirás.

El juramento de lealtad es una promesa de fidelidad o amistad a los Estados Unidos. Al repetir el juramento te conviertes en ciudadano estadounidense.

Los trámites de inmigración y naturalización son largos. Hay que tener paciencia. Si tienes más preguntas al respecto, comunícate con la Oficina de Inmigración más cercana. Está allí para ayudarte.

The oath of allegiance is a promise of loyalty, or friendship, to the United States. When you repeat the oath of allegiance, you become an American citizen.

The process of immigrating to America and becoming a naturalized U.S. citizen is a long one. It requires patience. If you have any other questions, contact the Immigration Office that is nearest to you. It is there to help you.

Offices of the Immigration and Naturalization Service

Oficinas del Servicio de Inmigración y Naturalización de los Estados Unidos

801 Pacific News Bldg.
P.O. Box DX
Agana, GU 96910

Room 220 U.S. Post Office
and Courthouse
445 Broadway
Albany, NY 12207

Federal Building, U.S.
Courthouse
701 "C" St., Rm. D-229
*Anchorage, AK 99513

Rm. 1408 Richard B. Russell
Federal Office Building
75 Spring St. S.W.
*Atlanta, GA 30303

E. A. Garmatz Federal
Building
100 South Hanover Street
*Baltimore, MD 21201

John Fitzgerald Kennedy
Federal Building
Government Center
*Boston, MA 02203

68 Court Street
*Buffalo, NY 14202

Charles R. Jonas Federal
Building
401 W. Trade St.,
P.O. Box 31247
Charlotte, NC 28231

Dirksen Federal Office
Building
219 South Dearborn St.
*Chicago, IL 60604

U.S. Post Office and
Courthouse
5th and Walnut Sts.
P.O. Box 537
Cincinnati, OH 45201

Anthony J. Celebrezze
Federal Building
1240 East 9th Street,
Room 1917
*Cleveland, OH 44199

U.S. Immigration and
Naturalization Service
Room 6A21, Federal Building
1100 Commerce St.
*Dallas, TX 75242

17027 Federal Office Building
*Denver, CO 80202

---

*Indicates District Office
Reprinted by permission from International Institute of Detroit.

36

Federal Building
333 Mt. Elliott Street
*Detroit, MI 48207

343 U.S. Courthouse
P.O. Box 9398
*El Paso, TX 79984

Federal Building, U.S.
  Courthouse
1130 "O" St.
Fresno, CA 93721

104 Federal Building
507 State Street
Hammond, IN 46320

719 Grimes Ave.
*Harlingen, TX 78550

900 Asylum Ave.
*Hartford, CT 06105

Federal Building
301 South Park
Room 512
*Helena, MT 59601

595 Ala Moana Boulevard
P.O. Box 461
*Honolulu, HI 96809

Federal Building
515 Rusk Avenue
P.O. Box 61630
*Houston, TX 77208

Rm. 227 Post Office Building
311 W. Monroe St.
P.O. Box 4608
Jacksonville, FL 32201

Suite 1100
324 E. Eleventh St.
*Kansas City, MO 64106

Federal Building, U.S.
  Courthouse
300 Las Vegas Blvd., South
Las Vegas, NV 89101

300 North Los Angeles Street
*Los Angeles, CA 90012

814 Federal Building
167 North Main Street
Memphis, TN 38103

Room 1324, Federal Building
51 S.W. First Avenue
*Miami, FL 33130

Rm. 186, Federal Building
517 East Wisconsin Avenue
Milwaukee, WI 53202

Federal Building
970 Broad Street
*Newark, NJ 07102

Postal Service Building
701 Loyola Avenue
*New Orleans, LA 70113

26 Federal Plaza
*New York, NY 10007

Norfolk Federal Building
200 Granby Mall, Rm. 439
Norfolk, VA 23510

Room 1008, New Federal
  Building
106 South 15th Street
*Omaha, NE 68102

Room 1321, U.S. Courthouse
Independence Mall West
601 Market Street
*Philadelphia, PA 19106

Federal Building
230 North First Avenue
*Phoenix, AZ 85025

2130 Federal Building
1000 Liberty Avenue
Pittsburgh, PA 15222

76 Pearl St.
*Portland, ME 04112

Federal Office Building
511 N.W. Broadway
*Portland, OR 97209

Federal Building, U.S. Post
   Office
Exchange Terrace
Providence, RI 02903

Suite 150
Rm. 1-060
630 Capitol Mall
Reno, NV 89502

Federal Building
P.O. Box 591
*St. Albans, VT 05478

Room 423, U.S. Courthouse
   and Customhouse
1114 Market Street
St. Louis, MO 63101

927 Main Post Office Building
180 E. Kellogg Blvd.
*St. Paul, MN 55101

Room 4103
New Federal Building
125 South State Street
Salt Lake City, UT 84138

U.S. Federal Building
727 East Durango
Suite A301
*San Antonio, TX 78206

880 Front St.
*San Diego, CA 92188

Appraisers Building
630 Sansome Street
*San Francisco, CA 94111

GPO Box 5068
*San Juan, PR 00936

701 W. 17th St.
Santa Ana, CA 92701

815 Airport Way, South
*Seattle, WA 98134

691 U.S. Courthouse
   Building
Spokane, WA 99201

500 Zack St., Rm. 539
Tampa, FL 33602

25 E. St., NW.
*Washington, DC 20538

Part Two

PREPARING FOR THE NATURALIZATION TEST

Segunda Parte

PREPARANDOTE PARA EL EXAMEN DE NATURALIZACION

EN la Segunda Parte aprenderás lo que tienes que saber sobre los Estados Unidos para poder aprobar el examen de ciudadanía. Consta de cinco capítulos. Cubren la historia norteamericana, la Constitución de los Estados Unidos, los gobiernos locales y de los condados, los gobiernos estatales y el gobierno federal o nacional. Cada capítulo tiene preguntas similares a las que te harán en el examen de ciudadanía.

La Tercera Parte es una sección especial que te ayudará a aplicarte un examen a tí mismo para que te des cuenta de lo que has aprendido. Esta sección viene en inglés solamente, puesto que presentarás el examen de verdad en ese idioma.

IN Part Two you will learn what you need to know about the United States in order to pass your citizenship exam. There are five chapters. They cover the history of the United States, the United States Constitution, local and county government, state government, and the federal government. Each chapter contains questions similar to the ones that you will be asked on the citizenship exam. Part Three is a special section that will help you test yourself to see how much you have learned.

1
La Historia de los Estados Unidos

¿Quién Descubrió América?

Cristóbal Colón descubrió América en el año 1492.

Colón era un cartógrafo italiano, o sea hacía mapas. Pensó que podía encontrar una ruta más corta a la China. En aquellos tiempos la gente europea ansiaba tener artículos traídos de la China pero llegar hasta allí en barco era difícil. Se demoraba mucho tiempo también. Colón estaba seguro que podía encontrar una ruta más fácil.

Llevó su idea a los Reyes de España, Fernando e Isabel. El 3 de agosto de 1492, Colón y un grupo de hombres valientes zarparon en tres naves pequeñas. Se llamaban la *Nina*, la *Pinta* y la *Santa María*.

Colón no descubrió nunca una ruta más corta a la China. Pero sí descubrió el Nuevo Mundo. El 12 de octubre de 1492 Colón llegó a la costa oriental de una de las Islas Bahamas. De allí siguió por las costas de Haití y Cuba. Se creía en la India y por eso llamó a las gentes de tez oscura que encontró "Indios." Hoy en día estas islas se llaman en inglés "Las Indias Occidentales."

1
History of the United States

Who Discovered America?

Christopher Columbus discovered America in 1492.

Columbus was an Italian navigator. He thought that he could find a short route to China. In those days, people were eager to have goods from China, but sailing there was difficult. It also took a long time. Columbus was sure he could find an easier way.

He took his idea to King Ferdinand and Queen Isabella of Spain. They gave him enough money to try to sail to China. On August 3, 1492, Columbus and a group of brave men set sail in three ships. They were called the *Nina*, the *Pinta*, and the *Santa Maria*.

Columbus never found a short route to China. Instead he discovered the New World. On October 12, 1492, Columbus reached the east coast of one of the Bahama Islands. From there, he sailed along the coasts of Haiti and Cuba. Columbus thought he was in India, so he called the dark-skinned people he met Indians. Today, these islands are called the West Indies. Columbus set sail three more times. On his fourth trip, he reached Central America.

Colón hizo tres viajes más. En el cuarto viaje llegó hasta la América Central.

Todos los años, se celebra el 12 de octubre como el Día de Colón. Esta fecha se conmemora también en el Canadá, México, Sur América, Centroamérica y España.

Every year, Americans celebrate Columbus Day on October 12. It is also celebrated in Canada, Mexico, South America, and Central America.

What Is the Capital of Your State?

You live in the United States of America. It is made up of fifty states. Listed below are the fifty states and their capitals.

¿Cuál Es la Capital de Tú Estado?

Vives en los Estados Unidos de Norteamérica. Hay cincuenta estados. A continuación hay una lista de los cincuenta estados y sus capitales.

STATE	CAPITAL
1. Alabama	Montgomery
2. Alaska	Juneau
3. Arizona	Phoenix
4. Arkansas	Little Rock
5. California	Sacramento
6. Colorado	Denver
7. Connecticut	Hartford
8. Delaware	Dover
9. Florida	Tallahassee
10. Georgia	Atlanta
11. Hawaii	Honolulu
12. Idaho	Boise
13. Illinois	Springfield
14. Indiana	Indianapolis
15. Iowa	Des Moines
16. Kansas	Topeka
17. Kentucky	Frankfort
18. Louisiana	Baton Rouge
19. Maine	Augusta
20. Maryland	Annapolis
21. Massachusetts	Boston
22. Michigan	Lansing
23. Minnesota	St. Paul
24. Mississippi	Jackson

STATE	CAPITAL
25. Missouri	Jefferson City
26. Montana	Helena
27. Nebraska	Lincoln
28. Nevada	Carson City
29. New Hampshire	Concord
30. New Jersey	Trenton
31. New Mexico	Santa Fe
32. New York	Albany
33. North Carolina	Raleigh
34. North Dakota	Bismarck
35. Ohio	Columbus
36. Oklahoma	Oklahoma City
37. Oregon	Salem
38. Pennsylvania	Harrisburg
39. Rhode Island	Providence
40. South Carolina	Columbia
41. South Dakota	Pierre
42. Tennessee	Nashville
43. Texas	Austin
44. Utah	Salt Lake City
45. Vermont	Montpelier
46. Virginia	Richmond
47. Washington	Olympia
48. West Virginia	Charleston
49. Wisconsin	Madison
50. Wyoming	Cheyenne

¿Cuáles Fueron las Trece Colonias Originales?

Cuando los pobladores europeos empezaron a llegar a América, vinieron de varios países europeos. Poblaron, o fundaron colonias. Una colonia es un territorio o un grupo de personas que mantiene sus lazos políticos con la Madre Patria. Los colonos generalmente pagan impuestos a la Madre Patria y se rigen por algunas de las mismas leyes.

La primera colonia británica en Norteamérica fue fundada por el Capitán John Smith en el año 1607. Llegados en barco desde Inglaterra, el Capitán Smith y sus hombres poblaron la colonia de Virginia. Vinieron al Nuevo Mundo en búsqueda de oro pero encontraron más bien una tierra fértil, apta para la agricultura.

En el año 1620, un barco llamado *Mayflower* (Flor de Mayo) zarpó de Inglaterra con un grupo de personas devotas llamadas "Peregrinos." El *Mayflower* arribó a la costa del actual estado de Massachusetts.

Cuatro años después, pobladores holandeses salieron de los Países Bajos y zarparon para América. Arribaron a la costa oriental norteamericana y fundaron la colonia de Nueva Amsterdam. Hoy en día es el estado de Nueva York.

Otro grupo de colonos devotos zarpó de Inglaterra durante los años 1628 a 1631. Se llamaban "Puritanos." Los Puritanos fundaron varias colonias en el nordeste, una región conocida como Nueva Inglaterra.

Poco despúes de la llegada de los Peregrinos, unos colonos suecos vinieron a América y poblaron lo que es hoy el estado de Delaware.

En 1681, otro grupo de devotos ingleses, llamados "Cuáqueros," vinieron a vivir al Nuevo Mundo. Fundaron una colonia que hoy es el estado de Pennsylvania. Su colonia tomó su nombre en honor a William Penn, un importante líder cuáquero.

What Were the Original Thirteen Colonies?

When settlers from Europe began to arrive in America, they came from many different places in Europe. They founded, or settled, colonies. A *colony* is a land or group of people that keeps its ties to a parent country. Colonists often pay taxes to the parent country, and they share some laws.

The first colony in America was settled by Captain John Smith in 1607. Sailing from England, Captain Smith and his men founded the colony of Virginia. They had come to the New World looking for gold, but instead they found rich land suitable for farming.

In 1620, a ship called the *Mayflower* sailed from England carrying a group of religious people called Pilgrims. The *Mayflower* landed in what is now the northeastern part of the United States. The Pilgrims founded several colonies in New England, as the region was soon called.

Four years later Dutch settlers left Holland and sailed for America. They landed on the eastern coast of America and in 1626 founded the colony of New Netherland. Today, it is the state of New York, and the former settlement of New Amsterdam is New York City.

Another group of religious settlers set sail from England during the years 1628 to 1631. They were called Puritans. The Puritans settled in what is now the state of Massachusetts.

Shortly after the Pilgrims arrived, Swedish people came to America and settled in what is now the state of Delaware.

In 1681, an English religious group, called Quakers, came to the New World to settle. They founded a colony in what is today the state of Pennsylvania. Their colony was named after William Penn, an important Quaker leader.

Ya para el año 1733 las trece colonias de la costa oriental del continente de Norte América pertenecían a Inglaterra. Cuando las colonias declararon su guerra de independencia contra los británicos, se convirtieron en los trece estados originales. Eran Delaware, Pennsylvania, Nueva Jersey, Georgia, Connecticut, Massachusetts, Maryland, Carolina del Sur, Nuevo Hampshire, Virginia, Nueva York, Carolina del Norte y Rhode Island. Las franjas blancas y rojas de la bandera estadounidense representan estos trece estados originales.

¿Cómo Consiguieron Su Independencia las Colonias?

Aunque los colonos gozaron de muchas libertades bajo el régimen británico, Inglaterra promulgó muchas leyes que los colonos tenían que obedecer. Estas leyes fueron aprobadas en Inglaterra donde no había representación oficial de las colonias. Más aún, los colonos tenían que pagar impuestos altos. Se pusieron cada vez más iracundos hasta que al fin decidieron que había que hacer algo.

En el año 1774 los colonos organizaron una gran reunión llamada el Primer Congreso Continental. Todas las colonias, menos Georgia, mandaron sus representantes. En el Congreso, los colonos decidieron pedirle al Rey de Inglaterra que les concediera plenos derechos como ciudadanos ingleses. El rey rechazó la petición.

Un año después, el Segundo Congreso Continental se reunió para decidir qué hacer frente a esta situación. Los representantes se reunieron en el Edificio de la Independencia en la ciudad de Filadelfia, estado de Pennsylvania. Los colonos decidieron que librarían una guerra para conseguir su independencia de Inglaterra.

By 1733, England owned all of the thirteen colonies that had been settled. When American declared its war of independence against the British, the thirteen colonies became the original thirteen states. They were Delaware, Pennsylvania, New Jersey, Georgia, Connecticut, Massachusetts, Maryland, South Carolina, New Hampshire, Virginia, New York, North Carolina, and Rhode Island. The stripes on the U.S. flag represent these original thirteen states.

How Did the Colonies Become Independent?

Although the colonists had many freedoms under British rule, England kept passing laws that the colonists were expected to follow. These laws were passed in England, where there were no government representatives of the colonies. Furthermore, the colonists were heavily taxed. They grew angrier and angrier, until they finally decided they had to do something.

In 1774, the colonists organized a large meeting, called the First Continental Congress. All the states except Georgia sent representatives. At the meeting, the colonists decided to ask the King of England to grant them full rights as Englishmen. The King refused to do so.

A year later, the Second Continental Congress met to decide what to do about the situation. The representatives gathered in Independence Hall, in Philadelphia, Pennsylvania. The colonists decided they would fight a war to win independence from England.

En enero de 1776, Thomas Paine escribió un panfleto con el título *Sentido Común*. Habló sobre la libertad y lo que podría significar para los colonos. Este panfleto causó mucho entusiasmo sobre la idea de la libertad para el país. En 1776, cuando se publicó la Declaración de Independencia, los colonos estaban dispuestos a luchar por la libertad.

Los hombres que escribieron la Declaración de Independencia fueron escogidos en el Segundo Congreso Continental. Thomas Jefferson escribió la mayor parte, pero le ayudaron Benjamín Franklin y John Adams. Los representantes del Segundo Congreso Continental firmaron el documento el día 4 de julio de 1776. Después de esta fecha, que se celebra todos los años, los colonos se consideraron como un pueblo libre, aunque claro está les tocó una guerra larga y dura con Inglaterra para ganar la libertad.

¿Qué Fue la Guerra Revolucionaria?

Cuando el Segundo Congreso Continental se reunió en mayo de 1775, se eligió a George Washington como comandante supremo del Ejército Continental. Aunque muchos colonos todavía sentían lealtad a Inglaterra, declararon la guerra.

Llegaron de muchos países personas que apoyaban la lucha por la libertad de los colonos. Los generales Lafayette y Rochambeau vinieron de Francia, como también el alemán llamado De Kalb; Kosciusko y Pulaski vinieron de Polonia; Von Steuben vino de Alemania para ayudar a Washington a entrenar y dirigir a los soldados.

En todo el país, hombres y mujeres colaboraron en el esfuerzo bélico. La mayoría de los hombres lucharon como soldados mientras que las mujeres se encargaron de los cultivos y el tejido de las telas para los uniformes de los soldados. Hubo muchos hombres y mujeres valientes en la Revolución Norteamericana o la Guerra de la Independencia, pues así también se le llama.

In January 1776, Thomas Paine wrote a pamphlet called *Common Sense*. He talked about freedom and what it would mean to the colonists. This pamphlet got people excited about becoming a free country. In 1776, when the Declaration of Independence was published, the colonists were ready to fight for their freedom.

The men who wrote the Declaration of Independence had been picked at the Second Continental Congress. Thomas Jefferson did most of the writing, but he was helped by Benjamin Franklin and John Adams. The representatives of the Second Continental Congress signed the document on July 4, 1776. After that date, which is celebrated today, the members of the colonies considered themselves a free people, although, of course, they fought a long, hard war with England to win their freedom.

What Was the Revolutionary War?

When the Second Continental Congress met in May 1775, they elected George Washington commander in chief of the Continental Army. Even though many colonists still felt loyalty to England, the colonists declared war on England.

People who supported the colonists' fight for freedom came from many countries to help. General Lafayette and Rochambeau came from France, as did a German man named De Kalb; Kosciusko and Pulaski came from Poland; and Von Steuben came from Germany to help Washington train and lead the soldiers.

Throughout the country, men and women helped in the war effort. Most of the men fought as soldiers, while the women farmed or wove material for soldier's uniforms. There were many brave men and women in the American Revolution or the War of Independence, as it was also called.

Aunque la Declaración de la Independencia se promulgó en 1776, la guerra continuó hasta el mes de octubre de 1781. Dos años después, Inglaterra firmó un tratado en el cual acordaba dejar libres las colonias norteamericanas. Ahora los Estados Unidos era ciertamente un país independiente.

¿Cómo Se Organizó el Nuevo País?

En el año 1787 fueron enviados nuevamente delegados a Filadelfia. Esta vez era para reorganizar el gobierno de su nuevo país.

Los representantes decidieron rápidamente que el gobierno existente bajo los Artículos de Confederación, sobre los cuales hablaremos luego, no podían servir al nuevo país. Así que empezaron a preparar una nueva constitución. Muchos líderes importantes colaboraron en esta tarea. Estos incluían a Alexander Hamilton, Benjamín Franklin, James Madison, James Wilson y Gouverneur Morris. George Washington fue electo Presidente de la Convención Constitucional.

Después de aprobar la Constitución, el próximo paso consistía en poner a funcionar al gobierno con la elección de un Presidente, un Vice-Presidente, y los congresistas. Aunque George Washington había esperado regresar a su hacienda en Virginia para dedicarse a sus cultivos, después de la guerra, ésto no le fue permitido. Su nuevo país lo quería como primer presidente.

Después de ser electo Presidente de los Estados Unidos, George Washington viajó desde su hacienda en Virginia a Nueva York, en ese entonces capital de los Estados Unidos. En todas las ciudades y aldeas en el camino, le festejaron con banquetes y fiestas y otras celebraciones que demostraron la adoración de su pueblo. La mayor parte del viaje

Although the Declaration of Independence was issued in 1776, the war continued until October 1781. Two years later, England signed a treaty in which they agreed to give up ownership of the American colonies. The United States had truly become an independent country.

How Did the New Country Get Organized?

In 1787, delegates were once again sent to Philadelphia—only this time, they were going to reorganize the government of their new country.

The representatives soon decided that the Articles of Confederation would not work for the new country, so they began to write a new constitution. Many important leaders worked on the Constitution, including Alexander Hamilton, Benjamin Franklin, James Madison, James Wilson, and Gouverneur Morris. George Washington was elected President of the Constitutional Convention.

After the Constitution was accepted, the next step was to put the government in working order by electing a President and Vice-President and members of Congress. Although George Washington had hoped to return to his farm in Virginia and be a planter after the war, this was not to be. His new country wanted him for its first president.

After his election as President of the United States, George Washington traveled from his plantation in Virginia to New York, which was then the capital of the United States. At every city and town along the way, he was honored with dinners and parties and other celebrations that showed how much the people admired him. He traveled by horseback for most of the trip, but when he got to New Jersey, he was met by a special boat decorated in red, white, and blue. Washington sailed into the New York

lo hizo a caballo, pero cuando llegó a Nueva Jersey, le esperó un barco especial decorado en rojo, blanco y azul. Washington entró al puerto de Nueva York en este barco, saludado por el tronar de cañones que celebraban su llegada. Era el comienzo de un nuevo gobierno.

George Washington fue tan adorado por sus compatriotas que aún hoy día es conocido como el Padre de la Patria.

¿Qué Es la Doctrina de Monroe?

La Doctrina de Monroe figura entre las primeras y más importantes declaraciones sobre la política externa que haya hecho un presidente norteamericano.

James Monroe, el quinto presidente de los Estados Unidos, elaboró la Doctrina de Monroe. Hay un artículo de la Constitución que obliga al Presidente que renda un informe cada año al Congreso sobre el estado de la Unión (o sea las condiciones del pais). Por costumbre, los presidentes han dado este informe anual en forma de un discurso.

La Doctrina de Monroe fue parte del Informe sobre el Estado de la Unión del Presidente Monroe en 1823. Fue una declaración importante por dos motivos. Primero, el Presidente declaró que los Estados Unidos no permitiría que ningún país europeo fundara colonias en las Américas. Pero, aún más importante, advirtió a los gobiernos europeos que no intervinieran contra ningún gobierno en las Américas.

Esta declaración importante sobre la política externa todavía está vigente hoy en día. Es tan importante para los norteamericanos ahora como era en 1823.

harbor on this boat to the sound of guns celebrating his arrival. It was the beginning of the new government.

George Washington was so beloved by his fellow Americans that he is known even today as the Father of the Country.

What Is the Monroe Doctrine?

The Monroe Doctrine was one of the first and perhaps the most important foreign policy statements ever made by an American president.

James Monroe, the fifth president of the United States, created the Monroe Doctrine. By the time Monroe was president, an article of the Constitution existed saying that the president should make a speech to Congress every year. This was called the State of the Union Address. It is still given today.

The Monroe Doctrine was part of President Monroe's State of the Union Address in 1823. It was an important statement for two reasons. First, the President declared that the United States would not let any foreign countries build colonies in the Americas. But more important, it warned other countries not to interfere with any government in the Americas.

This major foreign policy statement still stands today. It is just as important to Americans now as it was in 1823.

¿Cómo Fueron Creciendo los Estados Unidos?

La expansión de los Estados Unidos más allá de sus trece estados originales es una historia interesante. Se adquirieron de maneras diferentes nuevas tierras, algunas por medio de la conquista guerrera, otras por medio de la compra a gobiernos extranjeros. El primer estado que se adquirió después de la Guerra Revolucionaria fue Vermont, en el año 1791. Los más recientes fueron Alaska y Hawaii en 1959.

El territorio más grande adquirido en un momento de la historia fue el terrirorio de Luisiana, comprado a Francia en 1803. De esta "Compra de Luisiana" eventualmente salieron trece estados más.

Más adelante, el territorio de Texas, antes un país independiente, entró a la Unión en 1845. Por medio de un acuerdo con Inglaterra en 1846 se obtuvo otro territorio grande, el territorio de Oregón. En 1846, una guerra con México resultó en la adquisición de California. Por último, con una pequeña compra a México en 1853 se adquirieron partes de Colorado y Nuevo México.

En el momento de su adquisición muchos de estos territorios eran salvajes, sin población blanca. Sin embargo, los norteamericanos ansiaban ir a nuevas tierras y así el Oeste norteamericano se pobló rápidamente durante mediados del siglo diecinueve.

¿Qué Fue la Guerra Civil?

La Guerra Civil, o la Guerra entre los Estados según se denomina a veces, duró del año 1861 a 1865. El motivo de la guerra fue la esclavitud.

How Did the United States Grow?

How the United States expanded from its original thirteen colonies is an interesting story. New lands were added in many ways, some through war and some through purchases of lands from foreign governments. The first state added after the Revolutionary War was Vermont, in 1791. The most recent states to be added were Alaska and Hawaii in 1959.

The largest single land area, the Louisiana Territory, was added in 1803 when it was purchased from France. Thirteen states were carved out of the Louisiana Purchase.

After that, the Texas Territory, which had been an independent country, was added in 1845. The Oregon Territory, another large land mass, was obtained by treaty from England in 1846. In 1846, a war fought with Mexico brought California into the United States. Finally, a small purchase of land from Mexico in 1853 added parts of Colorado and New Mexico to the country.

When these lands were acquired, the territories were wild and often unsettled by white people. Americans, though, were eager to expand into new lands, so the American West was settled quickly during the last half of the nineteenth century.

What Was the Civil War?

The Civil War, or the War Between the States as it is sometimes called, lasted from 1861 to 1865. The war was fought over the question of slavery.

Los estados sureños permitían la esclavitud de los negros. Muchos Norteños y también muchos Sureños creían que la esclavitud no era aceptable moralmente. Al comenzar la Guerra Civil, había quince estados que permitían la esclavitud y había dieciocho estados que habían rechazado la esclavitud. Elegido Abraham Lincoln como Presidente de los Estados Unidos en 1860, muchas sureños se sintieron amenazados ya que sabían—que Lincoln estaba en contra de la esclavitud.

Dos grandes generales encabezaron los ejércitos. Robert E. Lee tuvo el mando del Ejército de la Confederación, así se llamaba el Sur durante la guerra, y Ulysses S. Grant dirigía el Ejército de la Unión, o sea el Norte.

La Guerra Civil fue la más terrible de su época. Hubo más de 750,000 bajas entre muertos y heridos. Fue también una época de rápido desarrollo industrial. Hubo una expansión notable de los ferrocarriles como también de las industrias del acero y las comunicaciones para respaldar el esfuerzo bélico.

Terminó la guerra con la rendición del General Lee. Poco después, murió el Presidente Lincoln víctima de un asesino, el actor John Wilkes Booth. Sin embargo, el país permaneció unido y se liberaron todos los esclavos.

¿Es Puerto Rico un Estado?

Puerto Rico no es un estado. Es más bien una república perteneciente a los Estados Unidos. Legalmente es un Estado Libre Asociado. Esto quiere decir que tiene lazos políticos y económicos con los Estados Unidos, pero tiene un gobierno elegido libremente y su propia cultura. Políticamente, los puertorriqueños gozan de los mismos dere-

The southern states owned black people as slaves. Many Northerners and also some Southerners felt that owning a human being was wrong. At the time of the Civil War, there were fifteen slave states and eighteen free states. When Abraham Lincoln was elected President in 1860, many Southerners felt threatened, since they knew he was against slavery.

Each army was led by a great general. Robert E. Lee headed the army of the Confederacy, as the South was called during the war, and Ulysses S. Grant headed the Northern army.

The Civil War was the worst war of its time. Over 750,000 men were killed or wounded. It was also a time of great industrial growth in the United States. Railroads, as well as the steel and communications industries, expanded greatly to support the war effort.

The war ended when General Lee surrendered. Shortly after the end of the Civil War, President Lincoln was assassinated by an actor named John Wilkes Booth. The country stayed united, however. The slaves, who had been freed before the end of the war by the Emancipation Proclamation, stayed free.

Is Puerto Rico a State?

Puerto Rico is not a state. Instead, it is a commonwealth of the United States. This means that it has political and economic ties to the United States, but it has its own government and culture. Politically, Puerto Ricans enjoy the same rights as U.S. citizens. Puerto Ricans who move to the United States can vote in elections if they meet local

chos que los ciudadanos norteamericanos. Los puertorriqueños residentes en los Estados Unidos pueden votar en las elecciones si cumplen los requisitos locales. Económicamente, los Estados Unidos han ayudado a Puerto Rico a industrializarse. Le han ayudado a desarrollar el turismo. Los puertorriqueños tienen un ingreso promedio menor al de los norteamericanos, pero mayor al de los demás latinoamericanos. Culturalmente, Puerto Rico está muy unido al resto de Latinoamérica.

requirements. Economically, the United States has helped Puerto Rico to become more industrialized. It has helped to build up tourism. Puerto Ricans still earn less than average Americans do, but they earn more than any other Latin American people. Culturally, Puerto Rico is very much like other Latin American countries.

2
La Constitución

¿Qué Eran los Artículos de Confederación?

En los momentos de publicar la Declaración de Independencia, algunos de los líderes coloniales decidieron que era preciso hacer un plan de organización para el nuevo gobierno. Decidieron que era una labor propia del Segundo Congreso Continental.

En junio de 1776, se nombró una comisión para elaborar un plan. En 1777, entró en vigencia el nuevo plan, llamado los Artículos de la Confederación.

Los Artículos de la Confederación se basaban en una "liga de amistad" entre los trece estados y establecieron un Congreso con igualdad de representación para todos los estados.

No tardaron en aparecer los problemas como resultado de los Artículos de la Confederación. Hubo querellas entre los estados por varios motivos. Los Artículos de la Confederación constituían una organización demasiado floja para mantener la unión de los estados. Hubo tres fallas principales. Primero, no existía un ejecutivo supremo para el

2
The Constitution

What Were the Articles of Confederation?

When the thirteen colonies were about to declare their freedom by issuing the Declaration of Independence, some of the leaders decided that a plan was needed to organize the new government. They decided this would be a good job for the Second Continental Congress.

In June 1776, a committee was created to write a plan to organize the government. In 1777, the new plan, called the Articles of Confederation, went into effect.

The Articles of Confederation declared the thirteen states to be in a "league of friendship." It set up a Congress with representatives from each state.

Soon there were problems with the Articles of Confederation. The states were quarreling among themselves over many issues. The Articles of Confederation were too weak to hold the new states together. They had three main weaknesses. First, there was no chief executive of the country. Second, there was no power to collect taxes from

país. Segundo, no había manera de implantar impuestos a los estados. Por último, no existía un mecanismo para solucionar los desacuerdos entre los estados.

Estuvieron vigentes los Artículos de Confederación hasta 1787, cuando fueron sustituídos por la Constitución.

¿Qué Es la Constitución de los Estados Unidos?

La Constitución que sustituyó a los Artículos de la Confederación viene a ser el fuero básico o ley suprema de los Estados Unidos. Establece la organización del gobierno y también contiene muchas leyes importantes.

La Constitución fue escrita en 1787 por los representantes de doce de los trece estados. El estado de Rhode Island fue el único que no cooperó. Fue escrita durante la Convención Constitucional celebrada en Filadelphia.

La Constitución explica y limita el poder del gobierno federal. Explica no sólo los poderes que pertenecen al pueblo sino también los poderes no atribuídos directamente al gobierno federal en la Constitución, los cuales pertenecen a los gobiernos locales y estatales. La Constitución estipula un jefe ejecutivo, el presidente, para dirigir el país. Concede al gobierno federal el poder de establecer impuestos. Establece una corte suprema para solucionar las disputas entre los estados.

La Constitución expresa ideas gubernamentales, nuevas en su época. Primero, divide el gobierno en tres ramas principales. Luego, dispone un sistema de restricciones y contrapesos mutuos para asegurar que haya equilibrio de poderes entre las ramas, sin dominio de una sobre otra.

Algunos ejemplos de esta característica del gobierno norteamericano son los siguientes:

the states. Finally, there was no way to settle arguments among the states.

The Articles of Confederation lasted until 1787, when they were replaced by the Constitution.

What Is the Constitution of the United States?

The Constitution, which replaced the Articles of Confederation, is the highest, or supreme, law of the United States. It is the plan for the organization of the government, and it also contains many important laws.

The Constitution was written in 1787 by representatives from twelve of the thirteen states. Only Rhode Island did not help. It was written at the Constitutional Convention held in Philadelphia.

The Constitution explains and limits the power of the federal government. It explains what powers belong to the people. Whatever powers are not given directly to the federal government in the Constitution belong to the states and the people. The Constitution provides for a chief executive to run the country. It gives the federal government the power to collect taxes. And it establishes a Supreme Court which settles arguments among the states.

The Constitution contains some new ideas about government. First, it divides the government into three branches. Then it provides a system of checks and balances to make sure that no one branch gains power over another.

Here are some of the checks and balances:

1. Los representantes de los poderes legislativo y ejecutivo son elegidos por el pueblo.
2. El Presidente puede vetar, o sea rechazar, una ley aprobada por el Congreso. Pero el Congreso puede superar el veto presidencial con otro voto.
3. La Corte Suprema dictamina sobre la legalidad o constitucionalidad de las leyes aprobadas por el Congreso.

Entonces puedes comprender que este sistema de restricciones y contrapesos mutuos existe para restringir el alcance del poder de cada uno de las tres ramas, pues así ninguna adquiere demasiados atributos, pero al mismo tiempo asegura que cada rama tenga suficiente poder para hacer contrapeso a las otras dos y así lograr el equilibrio.

Algunos estados no quisieron aceptar o ratificar la Constitución porque lo percibían como una falta de protección a los derechos individuales. Se les prometió a estos estados que se harían cambios o enmiendas a la Constitución para proteger los derechos del individuo. Ratificaron la Constitución. Para entrar en vigencia, era necesaria la ratificación de nueve estados. Quedó ratificada en 1788 y el nuevo gobierno empezó a funcionar en enero de 1789.

¿Cómo Está Dividida la Constitución?

La Constitución tiene tres divisions principales: un Preámbulo, siete artículos y veintiséis enmiendas. Las primeras diez enmiendas, conocidas como la "Declaración de Derechos," protegen los derechas de los ciudadanos. Dice así:

> Nosotros, el pueblo de los Estados Unidos, para formar una Unión más perfecta, establecer la justicia, asegurar la paz interna, hacer provisión para la defensa común, promover el bienestar general, y asegurar los frutos de la libertad para nosotros mismos y para nuestra posteridad, ordenamos y establecemos esta Constitución de los Estados Unidos de Norteamérica.

1. Representatives, including the chief executive, are elected by the people.
2. The President has veto power—that is, he can refuse to sign a bill Congress has passed. In turn, Congress can take another vote and remove his veto.
3. The Supreme Court rules on the legality of laws passed by Congress.

As you can probably see, checks and balances are used to check the power of any one branch of government so it does not gain too much control and to balance the power of each branch against the other two.

Some states did not want to ratify the Constitution because they felt the rights of individuals were not protected enough. These states were promised that amendments, or changes, would be made in the Constitution to protect individuals' rights. Then they ratified the Constitution. Nine states had to ratify the Constitution for it to be accepted. It was ratified in 1788. The new government officially began to operate in January 1789.

How Is the Constitution Divided?

The Constitution has a Preamble, three main divisions, seven articles, and twenty-six amendments. The first ten amendments, known as the Bill of Rights, protect the rights of individual citizens. The Preamble reads:

> We the people of the United States, in order to form a more perfect Union, establish justice, insure domestic tranquility, provide for the common defense, promote the general welfare, and secure the blessings of liberty to ourselves and our posterity, do ordain and establish this Constitution for the United States of America.

Los siete artículos explican cómo está dividido el gobierno federal en tres ramas y los parámetros de sus respectivos campos de acción. Las tres ramas son la legislativa, la ejecutiva, y la judicial. Aprenderás más sobre éstas, más adelante en este libro.

Los hombres que escribieron la Constitución, con gran sabiduría, se dieron cuenta que en el futuro sería necesario hacerle cambios y adiciones. Por consiguiente, incluyeron varias maneras para efectuar cambios en el documento original. Un cambio en la Constitución se llama una enmienda. Hay veintiséis hasta hoy. Los mismos autores de la Constitución escribieron las primeras diez enmiendas, conocidas en conjunto como la Declaración de Derechos, destinadas a proteger los derechos del ciudadano individual.

¿Qué Es la Declaración de Derechos?

La Declaración de Derechos protege los derechos y las libertades de todos los norteamericanos. Aquí tienes una breve explicación de la Declaración de Derechos, que consta de las diez primeras enmiendas a la Constitución.

La primera enmienda proteje y garantiza las libertades de palabra, de cultos y de prensa. Da al pueblo el derecho de hacer reuniones pacíficas, llamado la libertad de asamblea, y también el derecho de levantar peticiones al gobierno para cambiar las leyes.

La segunda enmienda garantiza el derecho de armarse. Algunos creen que así todo ciudadano puede tener un arma de fuego, mientras otros creen que así el pueblo puede mantener una milicia. Como ya ves, todavía se discute la interpretación de la Constitución.

La tercera enmienda declara que en épocas de paz no se les puede obligar a los ciudadanos que den alojamiento en sus casas particulares a los soldados del país.

The Preamble shows that it is the people themselves who are establishing the government.

The seven articles explain how the federal government is divided into three branches and describe the power that each branch has. These three branches are the legislative, the executive, and the judicial. You will learn more about these later.

The men who wrote the Constitution were wise enough to realize that changes or additions might be needed later. So they wrote in a way to change this document. A change in the Constitution is called an amendment. There have been twenty-six amendments so far. The first ten Amendments, called the Bill of Rights, were written by the authors of the Constitution.

What Is the Bill of Rights?

The Bill of Rights protects the rights and freedoms of all Americans. But this is only a short explanation of the Bill of Rights. The first ten amendments are the Bill of Rights.

The first amendment protects and guarantees freedom of speech, freedom of religion, and freedom of the press. It gives people the right to hold peaceful public meetings, which is called the right of assembly, and the right to petition the government to change laws.

The second amendment guarantees the right to bear arms. Some people think this means that every citizen is allowed to own guns, and others believe this means the people have a right to maintain a militia. As you can see, there is still a great deal of discussion even today about how the laws written into the Constitution are interpreted.

The third amendment states that private homes do not have to keep soldiers during times of peace.

71

La cuarta enmienda protege al ciudadano norteamericano contra las pesquisas y los asimientos ilegales. Por ejemplo, la policía no puede allanar una casa particular para buscar y tomar pertenencias como pruebas, al menos que tenga una orden judicial. Para conseguir esta orden tienen que explicar a un magistrado el objeto de la pesquisa proyectada y su relación con un supuesto crimen.

La quinta enmienda estipula varias protecciones ciudadanas. No se le puede hacer proceso judicial a una persona dos veces por el mismo crimen. No se le puede obligar a una persona a dar testimonio contra ella misma. No se le puede hacer proceso criminal a una persona a menos que haya sido sindicado por un jurado de acusación. No se puede privar a nadie de su libertad ni negarle sus derechos sin un proceso legal.

La sexta enmienda promete a todo ciudadano un proceso judicial rápido. Declara también que la persona tiene los derechos de saber de qué se le acusa, tener abogado, llamar testigos a su favor y oir los testigos en su contra.

La séptima enmienda afirma el derecho de proceso judicial con un jurado. Un jurado consiste de doce personas quiénes deciden la culpa o la inocencia de un acusado.

La octava enmienda estipula que a un acusado no se le puede cobrar ni fianza ni multa excesiva. Una fianza es una cantidad de dinero que un acusado consigna para no ir a la cárcel hasta el momento de su juicio. Tampoco no se le puede castigar de manera cruel o fuera de lo acostumbrado.

La novena enmienda asegura que la Declaración de Derechos no pretende ser una lista completa ni exhaustiva pero que se pueden agregar derechos.

La décima enmienda dice que cualquier poder que no se otorga al gobierno federal según la Constitución, entonces queda en manos de los estados o del pueblo.

The fourth amendment protects American citizens against illegal search and seizure. People's homes cannot, for example, be searched and their property taken as evidence unless the law officers have first gotten permission from a court to do so. To get this permission, they must tell a judge what they hope to find and how it is connected to a crime.

The fifth amendment provides several protections. No person can be tried twice for the same crime. No one can be forced to be a witness against himself. A person cannot be tried for a crime unless he has been accused of the crime by a grand jury.

The sixth amendment promises all citizens a speedy trial. It also states that a person must be told what crime he is accused of committing. He has a right to have a lawyer defend him. And he has a right to call witnesses in his defense, and also to hear the witnesses that speak against him.

The seventh amendment states that if a person is tried for a serious crime, he can have a trial by jury if he chooses to do so. A jury is a group of twelve persons who decide if an accused person is guilty or innocent.

The eighth amendment states that a person cannot be charged with too much bail or excessive fines. Bail is an amount of money that a person must pay in order to stay out of jail until the time of his trial. A person also cannot be given cruel or unusual punishment.

The ninth amendment assures that the Bill of Rights is not a complete list of rights, and that other rights may be added.

The tenth amendment says that whatever power the federal government is not given in the Constitution belongs to the states, or to the people.

Estas son las primeras diez enmiendas, llamadas la Declaración de Derechos.

¿Cómo Se Cambia la Constitución?

Para agregar una enmienda a la Constitución, se necesita dos turnos de votación.

Primero, dos tercios de ambas cámaras del Congreso tienen que proponer la enmienda. O se puede convocar a una convención nacional con el fin de proponer la enmienda. Para convocara una convención nacional, dos tercios de los estados tienen que estar a favor.

Segundo, tres cuartos de las asambleas legislativas de los cincuenta estados tienen que ratificar, o sea aprobar la enmienda, o tres cuartos de los estados tienen que ratificarla en convenciones estatales convocadas especialmente con ese motivo.

These are the first ten amendments, called the Bill of Rights.

How Can the Constitution Be Amended?

Before a new amendment can be added to the Constitution, two votes have to be taken.

First, either two-thirds of the members of both houses of Congress have to propose the amendment, or a national convention is called to propose the amendment. To call a national convention, two-thirds of the states must ask for it.

Second, either three-fourths of the legislatures in the fifty states must ratify, or approve, the amendment, or three-fourths of the states must ratify it at conventions held especially for that purpose.

3
El Gobierno Federal

¿Cuál Es la Capital de los Estados Unidos?

La capital de los Estados Unidos es la ciudad de Washington, D.C. Las letras "D.C." significan Distrito de Columbia, que no es un estado sino un distrito especial para la capital federal. George Washington escogió el lugar. Él creía que la capital federal no se debía situar en ninguno de los estados. Washington, D.C., es la novena ciudad de los Estados Unidos en términos de población. La tercera parte de sus habitantes son empleados del gobierno federal.

El Cerro del Capitolio queda en el centro de la ciudad. Sobre este cerro se erige el Capitolio, sede del Congreso. No se permite construir en Washington edificios más altos que el Capitolio.

Washington se enorgullece por sus museos y galerías de arte, sus iglesias y bibliotecas y, naturalmente, sus edificios gubernamentales.

De los muchos lugares de interés turístico en Washington, D.C., se destacan el Capitolio, la Corte Suprema, la Biblioteca del Congreso y los monumentos a Jefferson, Lincoln y Washington.

3

The Federal Government

What Is the Capital of the United States?

The capital of the United States is Washington, D.C. (District of Columbia). The District of Columbia is not a state. George Washington selected this spot. He felt that the capital should not be located in any of the states. Washington, D.C., is the ninth largest city in the United States. One out of every three people in Washington, D.C., works for the federal government.

Capitol Hill stands in the middle of the city. The Capitol, the building where Congress meets, sits on top of the hill. No building in Washington can ever be built any higher than the Capitol.

Washington is known for its museums, art galleries, churches, and libraries and, of course, its government buildings.

Among the many places to visit and sights to see in Washington, D.C., are the Capitol, the Supreme Court, the White House, the Library of Congress, and the Jefferson, Lincoln, and Washington memorials.

Aunque esta información no es necesaria para tu examen de naturalización, te puede interesar saber un poco sobre la capital de los Estados Unidos.

¿Qué Clase de Sistema Político Tienen los Estados Unidos?

Los Estados Unidos son una democracia y una república. Cuando se dice que es una democracia, el significado es un país libre. Pero es más preciso decir que es una república. En una república el pueblo elige sus representantes. Por medio de estos representantes el pueblo dirige al gobierno.

En la Peroración de Gettysburg, Abraham Lincoln caracterizó muy bien al gobierno. Dijo que el gobierno de los Estados Unidos es "del pueblo, por el pueblo y para el pueblo."

¿Cuáles Son las Tres Ramas del Gobierno Federal?

La Constitución divide al gobierno federal en tres ramas para ejercer los tres aspectos del poder: el poder legislativo, el poder judicial y el poder ejecutivo. El poder legislativo está en el Congreso. El Congreso crea las leyes. El poder ejecutivo las administra y las hace cumplir. El Ejecutivo lo encabeza el Presidente. El poder judicial está constituído por las cortes o tribunales. Su tarea es la de interpretar, o sea explicar, las leyes.

Cada una de estas tres funciones del gobierno son tratadas detalladamente a continuación.

Although you will not have to know about these things for your citizenship test, you still may enjoy knowing a little bit about the capital of the United States.

What Form of Government Does the United States Have?

The United States is both a democracy and a republic. When people say the United States government is a democracy, they mean that it is a free country. But it is more accurate to say that the government is a republic. In a republic, the people elect representatives. Through the representatives, the people run the government.

In the Gettysburg Address Abraham Lincoln described the government very well. He said that the United States government is "of the people, by the people, and for the people."

What Are the Three Branches of the Federal Government?

The Constitution divided the federal government into three branches: the legislative, the executive, and the judicial. The legislative branch is Congress. Congress makes the laws. The executive branch carries out the laws. It is headed by the President. The judicial branch is the court system. Its job is to interpret, or explain, the laws.

Each of these three parts of governments is discussed in careful detail below.

¿Cómo Está Organizado el Congreso?

La rama legislativa del gobierno federal es el Congreso. El Congreso está dividido en dos partes, o sea dos cámaras. Una es el Senado. La otra es la Cámara de Representantes o Diputados, que comúnmente la llaman la Cámara solamente.

La existencia de dos cámaras se basa en una buena razón. Asegura que todos los estados estén representados justa e igualmente.

El Senado consta de 100 senadores. Hay dos senadores por cada estado, sin tener en cuenta ni su extensión ni su población.

La Cámara de Representantes consta de 435 representantes. El número de representantes correspondiente a cada estado depende de la población de ese estado. Todo estado tiene por lo menos un representante.

Las dos cámaras tienen igualdad de poder para legislar, o sea, crear leyes. Pero cada cámara también tiene ciertos atributos que no tiene la otra.

Los senadores y los representantes deben ayudarte. Su labor no se limita a sus funciones en el Congreso. Son tus representantes ante el gobierno. Si tienes un problema con el Servicio de Inmigración o con cualquier otra entidad oficial, comunícate por medio de una carta o por teléfono con un senador de tu estado o con el representante de tu distrito.

¿Cómo Se Eligen los Senadores y Representantes?

Se eligen los senadores por seis años. Un senador debe tener por lo menos treinta años de edad. Debe ser ciudadano por un mínimo de nueve años y ser residente del estado que

How Is Congress Organized?

The legislative branch of the federal government is Congress. Congress is divided into two parts, or houses. One house is the Senate. The other is the House of Representatives, sometimes called the House.

There is good reason for having two houses. This insures that all states will be represented fairly and equally.

The Senate has 100 members called senators. There are two senators from each state, no matter how large or small the state is.

The House of Representatives has 435 members called representatives. The number of representatives depends on the number of people living in a state. Every state has at least one representative.

Both houses have equal powers to make laws. Each house also has some powers not given to the other.

Senators and representatives are supposed to help you. Their job is not limited to work they do in Congress. They are your government representatives. If you are having a problem with immigration, or with any part of government, you should write or call your senator or representative.

How Are Senators and Representatives Elected?

Senators are elected every six years. A senator must be at least thirty years old. He or she must have been an American citizen for nine years, and must be a resident of the

representa. Los senadores representan a toda la gente de su estado.

Se eligen los representantes cada dos años. Un representante tiene que haber cumplido veinticinco años. Debe ser ciudadano por siete años como mínimo y ser residente del estado que representa.

Los representantes se eligen en distritos electorales. Hay un representante para cada distrito. Todos los distritos tienen más o menos la misma población. Un representante es responsable a los habitantes de su distrito.

¿Cómo Funciona el Congreso?

La función principal del Congreso, claro está, consiste en crear las leyes del país. No obstante, el Congreso tiene muchas otras responsabilidades. Además, al Congreso se le prohibe hacer ciertas cosas. También hay funciones que corresponden a una de las dos cámaras y no a la otra.

Tanto senadores como representantes pueden votar en pro o en contra de todos los proyectos de ley y pueden presentar proyectos, menos los de levantar fondos. Solo los representantes pueden originar proyectos de ley que versan sobre los ingresos del gobierno, pero el Senado debe también aprobar el proyecto.

Sola la Cámara de Representantes puede acusar de mala conducta a los funcionarios del Ejecutivo o del Judicial, pero el Senado enjuicia al acusado. Solo el Senado aprueba a los funcionarios de alto nivel nombrados por el Presidente y también los tratados internacionales.

Ambas cámaras deben concurrir en destinar fondos para la defensa nacional. Pueden hacer lo necesario para mantener las fuerzas armadas. También pueden declarar guerras.

state he or she will represent. Senators represent everyone in the state.

Representatives are elected every two years. A representative must be twenty-five years old. He or she must have been an American citizen for seven years, and must be a resident of the state he or she will represent.

Representatives are elected from congressional districts. There is one representative from each congressional district. All congressional districts have about the same number of people in them. Each representative is responsible to the people in his or her district.

How Does Congress Work?

The main function of Congress, of course, is to pass laws. But Congress also has many other responsibilities. In addition, Congress cannot do certain things. And there are some things that only the Senate or only the House of Representatives may do.

Members of both houses may produce and vote on bills, which, if the President signs them, then become laws (except for bills to raise money). Only a member of the House of Representatives may start a bill that is intended to raise money, although senators may vote on the bill once it has been raised. Similarly, only the House may vote to bring a federal official to trial for crimes committed in office, but the trial must be held by the Senate. The Senate also has a right to approve the President's high appointees and the right to approve treaties.

Both houses of Congress are involved in providing money for overseeing the country's defense. They can do what is needed to maintain an armed forces. Both houses can also declare war.

Entre ambas se aprueba el recaudamiento de impuestos, el endeudamiento del gobierno, la reglamentación del comercio interno entre los estados y el internacional, la emisión de la moneda, el establecimiento de correos y el sistema uniforme de medidas, y la naturalización. También establecen todas las entidades necesarias para gobernar y servir al país.

Hay atributos prohibidos al Congreso. No puede imponer gravamen sobre las exportaciones ni crear leyes que favorezcan un estado sobre otro. No puede gastar dinero sin una ley anterior que fija el destino y la cuantía. Por último, el Congreso no puede crear una ley para castigar a un ciudadano por un acto que no era criminal en el momento que lo cometió, ni puede suspender los derechos legales de un acusado excepto en casos de guerra.

No hace falta recordar todas estas funciones, pero es importante tener ciertas nociones sobre ellas.

¿Quiénes Son los Dirigentes del Congreso?

El Vice-Presidente de los Estados Unidos desempeña la función del presidente del Senado. Tienes otras varias responsabilidades y no puede estar siempre presente en el Senado. Los Senadores eligen un presidente *pro tempore*, o sea encargado, para reemplazarlo durante sus ausencias.

El partido político que cuenta con el mayor número de senadores viene a ser el partido mayoritario del Senado. Los senadores de ese partido escogen su líder mayoritario y el segundo de éste, llamado "el cochero" (o azotador), pues trata de mantener la disciplina partitaria como el cochero

Both houses also can collect taxes and borrow money. They can regulate trade between the states. They can coin and print money.

Both houses are responsible for establishing the post office system and a uniform system of weights and measures. Both houses can pass laws about the process of naturalization. Both houses can establish any agencies and committees that are needed to run the government.

There are some things that neither the Senate nor the House of Representatives may do. Neither, for example, may tax exports. Neither can pass trade laws that favor one state over another. Neither house can spend money unless it has first passed a law telling how the money will be spent. Finally, Congress cannot pass a law to punish someone for something that was not a crime when the person committed the act. Congress is forbidden to interfere with a person's legal rights when someone has been accused of a crime.

You need not memorize all these functions, but it is important to know something about them.

Who Are the Officers in Congress?

The Vice-President of the United States is the president of the Senate. He has a lot of other responsibilities and cannot always be there, so the Senate elects a president *pro tempore* to take his place.

The political party in the Senate with the most people is called the majority party. The majority party has two leaders, called the majority leader and the majority whip. The majority leader is the elected leader of the party, and the whip helps to get votes for the programs of the party. The smaller party is called the minority party. It also has

pone a trabajar a sus caballos. El líder mayoritario es elegido líder del partido, y el cochero le ayuda a obtener votos para los programas del partido. El partido con menos senadores es el partido minoritario del Senado. Ellos eligen su líder minoritario y el "cochero" minoritario.

La Cámara de Representantes elige su presidente (o "el Orador") entre los mismos disputados. Tradicionalmente, pertenece al partido mayoritario de la Cámara. Cada partido, el mayoritario y el minoritario, tiene su líder y su "cochero."

¿Quién Puede Ser Presidente?

Para postularse como candidato a la presidencia de los Estados Unidos, el aspirante debe cumplir ciertos requisitos. Tiene que ser ciudadano nativo, o sea nacido en los Estados Unidos. Tiene que ser residente en el país por los catorce años anteriores como mínimo. Debe haber cumplido por lo menos treinticinco años de edad. Un presidente puede reelegirse sólo una vez, o sea no se permite más de dos turnos en la presidencia.

¿Cómo Se Eligen el Presidente y el Vice-Presidente?

Se eligen el Presidente y el Vice-Presidente cada cuatro años. El día señalado para las elecciones es el primer martes después del primer lunes del mes de noviembre. Sin embargo, se anuncian las candidaturas con mucha anticipación. En algunos estados se efectúan elecciones primarias anteriores a la elección nacional para que los partidos puedan empezar el proceso de eliminar los múltiples candidatos hasta llegar a uno para cada partido.

two leaders, called the minority leader and the minority whip.

The head of the House of Representatives is called the Speaker of the House. He is chosen by the House members. By tradition, he comes from the majority party. The House of Representatives also has a majority and minority party. Each party has its leader and whip.

Who Can Be President?

To run for president, a man or woman must meet certain qualifications. He or she must have been born in the United States. He or she must have lived here for the past fourteen years. He or she also must be at least thirty-five years old. No person can be elected president more than twice.

How Are the President and Vice-President Elected?

The President and Vice-President are elected every four years. Election Day is the first Tuesday after the first Monday in November. But long before the election, people from the political parties announce themselves as candidates. Some states have special elections, called primaries, to narrow down the candidates to just one person from each party.

Aunque existen algunos partidos pequeños, la política norteamericana es bipartidaria, o sea de dos partidos. Uno es el Partido Republicano, generalmente conservador. El otro es el Partido Demócrata, considerado más liberal.

Durante el verano anterior a las elecciones, los partidos se reúnen en grandes convenciones nacionales. En su convención, cada partido escoge un candidato presidencial. Los delegados provenientes de los estados donde se suele tener elecciones primarias llegan a la Convención comprometidos con uno u otro candidato. Otros delegados no tienen compromiso con ninguno. El partido apoyará al candidato seleccionado durante la campaña electoral. La convención ratifica también el segundo o el compañero de campaña nombrado por el candidato presidencial. Si triunfa éste en la elección, el compañero será el Vice-Presidente.

Durante los meses anteriores a la elección en noviembre, las campañas de los candidatos Republicano y Demócrata son intensas. Viajan a muchos estados del país para hacer discursos y hacerse conocer por el pueblo. Los dos candidatos a la presidencia pueden comparecer en la televisión para debatir las cuestiones básicas del momento.

En noviembre, los votantes concurren a las urnas electorales. Votan por su candidato predilecto a la Presidencia y por su compañero, candidato a la Vice-Presidencia.

Aunque el pueblo vota, no elige al Presidente y Vice-Presidente. A diferencia de los senadores y los representantes, elegidos por voto directo del pueblo de sus estados o sus distritos. El Presidente y el Vice-Presidente son elegidos por los miembros del Colegio Electoral.

Although there are some small parties, there are only two major parties in the United States. One is the Republican, or conservative, party. The other is the Democratic, or liberal, party.

In the summer of an election year, each party has a big national meeting called a convention. At the convention, each party picks one presidential candidate. This person is the choice of the party. The party will sponsor him or her. The presidential candidate picks a partner, called a running mate. If the candidate becomes President, the running mate will be Vice-President. States that had primary elections are already committed to a presidential candidate.

In the months before the election, both the Republican and Democratic candidates campaign very hard. They appear in many states, speaking to and meeting as many people as possible. The two candidates may appear publicly together on television so they can argue and discuss issues. This is called a debate.

In November, people go to the polls, as voting places are called. They vote for who they want as President and Vice-President.

Although the people vote for President and Vice-President, they do not actually elect them. Unlike senators and representatives, who are elected by a direct vote of the people, the President and Vice-President are chosen by the members of the electoral college.

¿Cómo Funciona el Colegio Electoral?

Cuando los votantes van a las urnas electorales para votar por su candidato preferido a la Presidencia, en realidad están eligiendo a unos electores, o sea los miembros del Colegio Electoral. El número de electores que le corresponde a cada estado es igual al total de sus senadores y representantes en el Congreso.

Al cierre de las urnas, se hace un conteo del voto popular. En cada estado por separado, el candidato con la mayoría de votos gana la totalidad de los electores de ese estado. Se hace una reunión de los electores en cada estado y éstos votan unánimemente por el candidato que obtuvo la mayoría en el estado. Los electores, compartidarios del candidato, están comprometidos a votar según el voto popular en su estado. Así funciona el Colegio Electoral.

En enero, el Congreso se reúne para contar oficialmente los votos de los electores. Se necesita una mayoría absoluta, o sea la mitad más uno. Si ningún candidato presidencial logra una mayoría absoluta, la Cámara de Representantes elige al Presidente votando por estados no como diputados individuales. Si ninguno logra una mayoría para Vice-Presidente, el Senado lo elige.

Algunas personas quieren mantener el sistema del Colegio Electoral. Otras personas quieren cambiar el sistema a un voto popular director porque el Presidente y el Vice-Presidente deben ser responsables directamente al pueblo.

¿Quién Puede Ser Votante?

La décimoquinta enmienda a la Constitución, ratificada después de la Guerra Civil, afirma que a nadie se le puede negar el derecho a votar por razón de la raza o el color de la piel, ni por haber sido anteriormente esclavo. La déci-

How Does the Electoral College Work?

When the voters go to the polls to vote for President and Vice-President, they are actually voting for electors, or special representatives. Each state is entitled to as many electors as it has senators and representatives.

After the polls close, the popular vote is counted. Whichever party has gotten the most votes wins the election. Its electors gather at a state meeting to vote for President and Vice-President. The electors are pledged to vote for the candidates who got the most votes in the state. This is known as the electoral college system.

In January, when Congress meets, it officially counts the votes of the electors. A majority is needed. If there is no majority—that is, if there is a tie—the House of Representatives votes for President. If there is a tie for Vice-President, they also vote for him.

Some people like the electoral college system, but other people think it should be changed so voters can elect the President and Vice-President directly, as they do their senators and representatives.

Who Can Vote?

The fifteenth amendment, which was passed after the Civil War, says that no one can be denied the right to vote because of race, color, or because he was once a slave. The

monovena enmienda, ratificada en 1920, concede el derecho de votar a la mujer.

Cualquier ciudadano, mayor de 18 años, puede votar en las elecciones presidenciales, o más bien, federales. Pero los estados y gobiernos locales pueden fijar ciertos requisitos para las otras elecciones. El más común es el de residencia. Para cumplir con el requisito de residencia, tienes que llevar un cierto tiempo viviendo en un estado o ciudad, de trienta a noventa días por lo general, antes de poder ser votante. Según la vigésimosexta enmienda a la Constitución, la edad mínima para votar es 18 años. Algunos estados requieren que los votantes sepan leer y escribir, pero no lo pueden hacer sino para las elecciones estatales y locales. Si alguien trata de negarte el derecho de votar a raíz de tus habilidades de leer y escribir, debes hablar con un funcionario para asegurarte que no se te está negando ese derecho sin justa causa. Por último, los estados pueden obligarte a inscribirte en las listas de votantes antes de poder ejercer el derecho al voto. Por lo general, debes inscribirte un cierto tiempo anterior a una elección, de costumbre unos treinta días. Al inscribirte, tienes que haber cumplido ya el requisito de residencia en el caso de que haya tal requisito.

Además de votar por el Presidente y el Vice-Presidente, se emplea el voto para decidir otras cosas también. Puedes elegir los senadores y representantes para el Congreso y también para la legislatura estatal. Puedes elegir los jueces locales. Puedes tal vez votar para aumentar o bajar los impuestos o a destinar unos ingresos para ciertos fines. Puede ser que te toque votar por alguna enmienda a la constitución federal o estatal, o decidir otras muchas cuestiones.

Votar es una responsabilidad muy seria y así la tienes que

nineteenth amendment, passed in 1920, guarantees women the right to vote.

Any U.S. citizen over 18 years old can vote in a federal election, that is, for President or Vice-President, but states and local governments can have certain requirements for other elections. The most common one is a residency requirement. To meet a residency requirement, you must have lived in a state or town for a certain period of time, usually thirty to ninety days, before you are allowed to vote in local or state elections. According to the twenty-sixth amendment, the voting age is 18. Some states require that you be able to read or write in order to vote, but this is only for local and state elections. If anyone ever tries to stop you from voting because of your reading and writing skills, you should talk to someone about this to be sure you have not been unfairly denied the right to vote. Finally, states can require that you register, or sign up, before you vote. Often, you must register a certain amount of time before an election, usually about thirty days. When you register in most states, you must have met the residency requirement if there is one.

In addition to voting for President and Vice-President, there are many other things to vote for. You can elect senators and representatives to Congress and also to your state legislative body. You may elect local judges. You may vote to raise or lower taxes or to spend money in a certain way. You may vote for federal or local amendments, and many other issues.

Voting is an important responsibility. You should take your voting responsibilities very seriously. To prepare for voting, try to learn as much as possible about the candidates. You can do this by talking to people, by reading newspapers and magazines, by watching television and

considerar. Para prepararte antes de votar, trata de informarte al máximo posible sobre los candidatos. Esto lo puedes hacer mediante la prensa, la televisión y la radio. También puedes estudiar los panfletos de los varios candidatos, pero, naturalmente, cada candidato sólo te cuenta los puntos a tu favor. Lo más importante es pensar antes de votar; así serás un votante serio.

listening to the radio. You can also read the campaign literature the candidates give you, but of course, each candidate will only tell you good things about himself or herself. The most important thing is to think before you vote—that makes you a serious voter.

Who Have Been the Presidents of the United States?

So far, forty men have been President of The United States.

¿Quiénes Han Sido los Presidentes de los Estados Unidos?

Hasta la fecha, cuarenta hombres han sido Presidente de los Estados Unidos.

PRESIDENT	INAUGURATED	PARTY
1. George Washington	1789	Federalist
2. John Adams	1797	Fed.
3. Thomas Jefferson	1801	Democrat-Republican
4. James Madison	1809	Dem.-Rep.
5. James Monroe	1817	Dem.-Rep.
6. John Quincy Adams	1825	Dem.-Rep.
7. Andrew Jackson	1829	Dem.
8. Martin Van Buren	1837	Dem.
9. William Henry Harrison	1841	Whig
10. John Tyler	1841	Whig
11. James K. Polk	1845	Dem.
12. Zachary Taylor	1849	Whig
13. Millard Fillmore	1850	Whig
14. Franklin Pierce	1853	Dem.
15. James Buchanan	1857	Dem.
16. Abraham Lincoln	1861	Rep.
17. Andrew Johnson	1865	Dem.-Rep.
18. Ulysses S. Grant	1869	Rep.
19. Rutherford B. Hayes	1877	Rep.
20. James A. Garfield	1881	Rep.
21. Chester A. Arthur	1881	Rep.
22. Stephen Grover Cleveland	1885	Dem.
23. Benjamin Harrison	1889	Rep.

PRESIDENT	INAUGURATED	PARTY
24. Stephen Grover Cleveland	1893	Dem.
25. William McKinley	1897	Rep.
26. Theodore Roosevelt	1901	Rep.
27. William Howard Taft	1909	Rep.
28. Thomas Woodrow Wilson	1913	Dem.
29. Warren G. Harding	1921	Rep.
30. John Calvin Coolidge	1923	Rep.
31. Herbert C. Hoover	1929	Rep.
32. Franklin Delano Roosevelt	1933	Dem.
33. Harry S. Truman	1945	Dem.
34. Dwight D. Eisenhower	1953	Rep.
35. John F. Kennedy	1961	Dem.
36. Lyndon B. Johnson	1963	Dem.
37. Richard M. Nixon	1969	Rep.
38. Gerald R. Ford	1974	Rep.
39. Jimmy (James Earl) Carter, Jr.	1977	Dem.
40. Ronald Reagan	1981	Rep.

¿Qué Hace el Jefe Ejecutivo?

El Presidente es el funcionario ejecutivo supremo del gobierno federal o nacional. Representa a todos los norte-americanos. El Artículo Segundo de la Constitución requiere la elección de un presidente que lleve a cabo las leyes del país. Sus atributos y sus obligaciones se detallan en la Constitución. Sin embargo, a través de los años, el Congreso ha aprobado leyes sobre los poderes y los deberes del Presidente.

El Presidente tiene poder en tres campos de acción principales. Dirige la rama ejecutiva, ejerce funciones legislativas y judiciales para mantener el equilibrio de poderío de las tres ramas del gobierno y maneja las relaciones con el exterior.

El deber principal del Presidente es el de llevar a cabo las leyes. Para cumplir con esta obligación, puede nombrar a los funcionarios federales. Nombra los Secretarios o Ministros del Gabinete, los embajadores y otros altos funcionarios. Ya que hay tantos cargos para llenar, y el Senado debe dar su aprobación a los nombramientos, el Presidente consulta frecuentemente con los senadores antes de hacer importantes nombramientos. A veces un senador le sugiere a una persona para cierto cargo y el Presidente lo acata. A pesar de la ayuda que le prestan los funcionarios nombrados, el Presidente es el responsable supremo de todos los departamentos, agencias, juntas y comisiones federales.

El Presidente colabora en las labores del Congreso. Por ejemplo, él puede proponer leyes al Congreso. También puede presionar a los Congresistas sobre los proyectos de ley que le son importantes. Y, por último, él firma un proyecto aprobado por el Congreso para así ponerlo en vigencia como ley. También puede rehusar firmarlo y ejerce su

What Does the Chief Executive Do?

The President of the United States is the chief executive officer of the federal government. He represents all Americans. Article II of the Constitution states that a president shall be elected to carry out all the laws. The President's powers and duties come from the Constitution. Over the years, though, Congress has also passed laws about his powers and duties.

The President has power in three main areas. He has lawmaking authority, judicial authority, and authority over foreign relations.

His main duty is to carry out the laws. To help carry out the laws, the President has the power to appoint federal officials. He names ambassadors and other high government officials. Because there are so many officials, he often consults with the senators before he makes major appointments. Sometimes, a senator suggests an appointment to him, and he accepts it. The President is also in charge of all federal agencies, departments, boards, and commissions.

The President can help make laws. For example, he can suggest laws to Congress. He can also talk with members of Congress about bills that are important to him. Finally, his lawmaking authority permits him to sign bills passed by Congress. He can also refuse to sign bills into law. This is called a veto. A veto is a strong power of the President. Sometimes, he only has to mention that he will veto a certain bill, and Congress will decide not to pass it.

Although the President can address Congress any time he wants to do so, he is required to make a special speech once a year. This is called the State of the Union speech. The President goes to the Capitol to give the speech every January when Congress opens its new session. If there is an

poder de veto. El veto es poderoso. A veces con sólo decir que vetaría tal proyecto, el Congreso no lo aprueba.

Aunque el Presidente puede dirigirse al Congreso en cualquier momento, es obligación hacerlo sólo una vez al año. Es para hacer su informe sobre las condiciones del país y por tradición se entrega el informe en un discurso llamado la Peroración sobre el estado de la Unión. El Presidente va al Capitolio al comienzo de cada año al inaugurar sus sesiones el Congreso en enero. Si hay una emergencia u otra razón especial, el Presidente puede convocar una sesión especial del Congreso.

La autoridad judicial del Presidente rige sobre los tribunales federales. Nombra a los magistrados de la Corte Suprema de Justicia y demás jueces de las cortes federales inferiores, con la aprobación del Senado. También puede conceder un indulto o suspender el castigo a una persona sentenciada en una corte federal. Sin embargo, no lo puede hacer para las personas con sentencias de las cortes estatales ni para los funcionarios federales enjuiciados por el Senado.

El último campo de poder del Presidente es la dirección de la política exterior. Mediante el Secretario de Estado (equivalente al Ministro de Relaciones Exteriores de otros países) y los embajadores, el Presidente maneja las relaciones con los otros países del mundo. Puede llegar a acuerdos ejecutivos. Negocia los tratados internacionales, pero el Senado los tiene que aprobar. El Presidente también lleva a cabo los términos de los tratados. Si le es necesario, puede recurrir a las fuerzas militares para hacer cumplir las leyes y llevar a cabo los tratados. El Presidente es el Comandante Supremo de las fuerzas armadas.

Por último, El Presidente también tiene el poder de declarar un estado de emergencia en los Estados Unidos. Esto podría ocurrir si surge alguna situación que sea un peligro para la nación o para alguna parte de ella.

emergency or special reason, he can call Congress into a special session.

The President's judicial authority is over the federal courts. He appoints the judges of the Supreme Court and federal judges, although the Senate must approve his appointments. The President can also grant a pardon or reprieve to any person who has been tried in a federal court. He may not, however, pardon persons tried in state courts, nor can he pardon a federal official who has been tried, or impeached, by the Senate.

The last important power of the President is to make foreign policy. Through the Secretary of State and the ambassadors, the president handles contacts with other countries. He can make executive agreements. He also works out treaties, but the Senate must approve them. The President also carries out treaties. If necessary, he may use the military to help him enforce laws and carry out treaties. The President is the Commander in Chief of the armed forces.

Finally, the President also has the power to declare a state of emergency in the United States. This might happen if any situation arose that could be dangerous to the entire country or to some section of it.

¿Cuándo Toma el Mando un Presidente?

El Presidente toma posesión de su cargo al mediodía del día 20 de enero siguiente a las elecciones. La ceremonia especial para la toma del mando se llama la inauguración. Se efectúa tradicionalmente en el costado del Capitolio. La familia presidencial, sus amigos, representantes de los estados y funcionarios del gobierno, incluyendo el Congreso, se congregan para la ceremonia. En todo el país el pueblo presencia la ceremonia por televisión.

El Presidente de la Corte Suprema de Justicia toma el juramento especificado por la Constitución:

> "Juro solemnemente que ejecutaré cabalmente las funciones del Presidente de los Estados Unidos y que haré todo lo que me sea posible para conservar, proteger y defender la Constitución de los Estados Unidos."

Después de la ceremonia de toma del mando, el Presidente y su familia se mudan al número 1600 de la Avenida Pennsylvania en Washington, D.C.—la Casa Blanca. Es la única casa en la cuadra. La Casa Blanca es propiedad de la nación y sirve de hogar para cada nuevo Presidente. Es además la sede presidencial.

¿Qué Es el Gabinete Presidencial?

Uno de los primeros actos del primer Congreso fue autorizar un grupo de ayudantes para el Presidente. Este grupo de ayudantes se llama el Gabinete. Muchos gobiernos tienen gabinetes de ministros que ayudan al jefe de gobierno en sus labores.

Los miembros del Gabinete, que se llaman Secretarios en los Estados Unidos, encabezan grandes departamentos (o ministerios). Se necesitan muchas personas para poner a

102

When Does the President Take Office?

The President takes office at 12 noon on the 20th of January following the election. The special ceremony that is held is called the inauguration. The new President is inaugurated on the east steps of the Capitol. His family, friends, representatives from the states, and many government officials, including members of Congress, gather to watch. People across the country watch the ceremony on television.

The Chief Justice of the Supreme Court says the oath required by the Constitution, and the President repeats it:

> "I do solemnly swear that I will faithfully execute the office of President of the United States, and will, to the best of my ability, preserve, protect, and defend the Constitution of the United States."

After the President is inaugurated, he and his family move into 1600 Pennsylvania Avenue in Washington, D.C.—the White House. It is the only house on the block. The White House belongs to the government, and it serves as home to each president.

What Is the President's Cabinet?

One of the first things Congress did was to arrange for a group to help the President carry out his many responsibilities. The group that helps the President is called the Cabinet. Many governments have Cabinets to help their chief executive carry out his work.

The members of the Cabinet, who are called Secretaries, each head a large department. Many people are needed to

funcionar cada departamento. Los departamentos gubernamentales son responsables del funcionamiento diario del
gobierno. Dan al Presidente la información necesaria para
que se mantenga al día.

De vez en cuando hay necesidad de crear un nuevo
departamento, y a veces un departamento se divide en dos
(porque es demasiado grande) para funcionar bien. Hoy en
día existen los siguientes departamentos gubernamentales:

Departamento de Agricultura
Departamento de Comercio
Departamento de Defensa
Departamento de Educación
Departamento de Energía
Departamento de Salud y Servicios Humanos
Departamento de Vivienda y Desarrollo Urbano
Departamento del Interior
Departamento de Justicia
Departamento de Trabajo
Departamento de Estado
Departamento de Transporte
Departamento de Hacienda

¿Cuáles Son las Responsabilidades del Vice-Presidente?

Si el Presidente queda incapacitado, muere, renuncia o
resulta condenado en un juicio ante el Senado, el Vice-
Presidente toma el mando como Presidente. Es el deber
más importante del Vice-Presidente—estar preparado para
reemplazar al Presidente. Hasta ahora, un Vice-Presidente
ha reemplazado a un Presidente nueve veces.

Muchas veces el Vice-Presidente representa al Presidente
en reuniones importantes y acontecimientos especiales.

Es también el Presidente del Senado, aunque no desempeña esta función con frecuencia. Sin embargo, el voto de
él es necesario cuando haya un empate.

run each department. Government departments are responsible for the day-to-day running of the government. They give the President the information he needs to keep informed about the government.

From time to time, a new department is needed, and sometimes a department is split into several departments because it has become too large to work properly. Today, there are the following government departments:

Department of Agriculture
Department of Commerce
Department of Defense
Department of Education
Department of Energy
Department of Health and Human Services
Department of Housing and Urban Development
Department of Interior
Department of Justice
Department of Labor
Department of State
Department of Transportation
Department of Treasury

What Are the Duties of the Vice-President?

If the President becomes disabled, dies, resigns or is convicted in an impeachment trial, the Vice-President becomes President. That is the Vice-President's most important duty—to stand by for the President. So far, a Vice-President has replaced a President nine times in American history.

The Vice-President often represents the President at important meetings throughout the country.

He is also the President of the Senate, although he does not often perform this duty. He is sometimes called upon, though, to vote in the Senate to break a tie.

Las condiciones que debe cumplir para ser elegible y la duración del cargo son las mismas de la presidencia.

¿Qué Pasaría Si el Presidente No Puede Desempeñar Sus Funciones?

Según la vigésimoquinta enmienda a la Constitución, en el caso de que el Presidente no pudiese desempeñar sus funciones o deja el mando por el motivo que sea, el Vice-Presidente lo reemplaza.

Si el Presidente se enferma a tal punto que no puede trabajar, él envía una carta al Presidente *pro tempore* del Senado y al Presidente de la Cámara de Representantes, para informarles que no puede seguir en el mando. Les pide luego que nombren al Vice-Presidente como Presidente Encargado hasta que pueda reasumir sus responsabilidades.

El Vice-Presidente con una mayoría del Gabinete también pueden decidir si el Presidente no está en condiciones para seguir en el mando y piden a los mismos dirigentes del Congreso que nombren al Vice-Presidente como Presidente Encargado.

Si el Vice-Presidente reemplaza al Presidente, uno de sus primeros actos es nombrar un nuevo Vice-Presidente.

Si algo ocurre que impida que el Vice-Presidente tome el mando, la persona que se elevaría a la presidencia es, en este órden:

Presidente de la Cámara de Representantes
Presidente *Pro Tempore* del Senado
Secretario de Estado
Secretario de Hacienda
Secretario de Defensa
Procurador General

The qualifications and term of office for the Vice-President are the same as for the President.

What Happens if the President Cannot Perform His Duties?

According to the twenty-fifth amendment of the Constitution, if the President cannot perform his duties, or is removed from office for any reason, or resigns, the Vice-President takes over for him.

If the President becomes too ill to work, he sends a letter to the President *pro tempore* of the Senate and to the Speaker of the House of Representatives telling them that he cannot continue as President. He asks them to appoint the Vice-President as Acting President until he is able to resume his duties.

The Vice-President and a majority of the Cabinet officers can also decide that the President is unable to carry out his duties, and they can ask that the Vice-President be made Acting President.

If the Vice-President becomes the President, one of his first acts is to appoint a new Vice-President who must also meet the approval of Congress.

If anything should happen to the Vice-President to keep him from performing as President, the persons next in line for the presidency would be:

Speaker of the House of Representatives
President *Pro Tempore* of the Senate
Secretary of State
Secretary of the Treasury
Secretary of Defense
Attorney General

¿Qué Es la Corte Suprema de Justicia?

La Constitución creó la Corte Suprema. Sirve para mantener el equilibrio de poderes con las otras dos ramas del gobierno. Controla el poder de éstas y protege los derechos del individuo y de los estados ante el poderío del Congreso y sus leyes y del Presidente y sus departamentos administrativos.

La Corte Suprema cumple su misión en dos maneras. Primero, puede declarar inconstitucional, o sea ilegal o carente de validez, una ley aprobada por el Congreso. Puede hacer lo mismo con los actos y reglamentos del Presidente y todos los demás funcionarios del Ejecutivo. Segundo, puede interpretar y aplicar las leyes y los reglamentos.

La mayoría de las causas que ve la Corte Suprema llegan en apelación de las cortes inferiores. Se hace una apelación cuando un interesado no acepta la decisión de una corte inferior y quiere que la Corte Suprema vea su causa. Por supuesto, la Corte Suprema no alcanza a oír todos las casos que solicitan su consideración. Sólo ven unos cien casos al año.

En algunos casos, la Corte Suprema es el tribunal de primera instancia. En estos casos la Corte Suprema tiene que ver el caso por ser el único tribunal autorizado. Un ejemplo de esto son los pleitos en que se ven involucrados los diplomáticos extranjeros.

La decisión emitida por la Corte Suprema es terminante. No hay más apelación después de la Corte Suprema de Justicia.

What Is the Supreme Court?

The Supreme Court was created by the Constitution. It serves to check and balance the powers of Congress. Since Congress has such broad powers to make laws, the Supreme Court can help control the power of Congress and make sure it does not interfere with individual or state rights.

There are two ways that the Supreme Court can do this. First, it can declare a law passed by Congress unconstitutional, or illegal. Second, it can interpret the laws Congress passes.

Most of the cases that are heard by the Supreme Court come from lower courts. They come to the Supreme Court on appeal. An appeal is made because someone does not like a decision made by a lower court and wants to hear what the Supreme Court has to say about it. Of course, the Supreme Court cannot possibly hear every case. It only hears about a hundred cases each year.

Sometimes the Supreme Court has what is called original jurisdiction. This means that it must hear a case. For example, the Court must hear cases involving foreign diplomats.

Whatever the Supreme Court decides is final. There is no appeal after the Court has ruled on something.

¿Qué Es el Sistema de Tribunales Federales?

Además de la Corte Suprema, existe un sistema nacional de tribunales divididos entre cortes federales a nivel de distrito y cortes federales regionales de apelación. En el país hay cien cortes distritales y diez cortes regionales de apelación. Existen también tribunales federales especializados para ver casos tales como los referentes a los patentes y a la aduana, y las apelaciones de las cortes militares. Aparte de estas cortes especiales, los tribunales federales sólo ven casos con base en las leyes federales, pleitos entre los estados y los entre un ciudadano norteamericano y un país extranjero.

El Presidente nombra a todos los magistrados y jueces del sistema federal de cortes, con el visto bueno del Senado.

¿Quiénes Son los Magistrados de la Corte Suprema?

Nueve jueces o magistrados forman la Corte Suprema. Uno es el Presidente de la Corte y los otros son Asociados.

Son nombrados como magistrados vitalicios por el Presidente de los Estados Unidos.

El Presidente nombra un nuevo magistrado de la corte sólo cuando alguien se retira o renuncia o muere. El Presidente envía al Senado el nombre de la persona que le parece la más indicada para formar parte de la Corte. Por lo general, el Senado acepta la selección presidencial. Pero si no la acepta, el Presidente tiene que buscar a otra persona para el cargo.

Una vez nombrado y aprobado, el nuevo Magistrado de la Corte Suprema presta juramento a cumplir con sus responsabilidades y a defender la Constitución.

What Is the Federal Court System?

In addition to the Supreme Court, the federal court system is divided into federal district courts and federal circuit courts of appeal. There are a hundred district courts and ten courts of appeal. There are also federal courts to handle specialized cases such as patents and customs and military appeals. Apart from these specialized courts, federal courts hear only cases involving federal laws, cases between states, and those involving foreign countries and an American citizen.

Judges in the federal court system are appointed for life by the President, with the Senate's approval.

Who Are the Supreme Court Judges?

There are nine judges, or justices, of the Supreme Court. One person is the Chief Justice and the others are Associate Justices.

Justices are appointed for a life term by the President.

The President names a new justice only when one retires, resigns, or dies. The President sends the name of the judge he wants to the Senate. Usually, the Senate votes in favor of the President's choice. If the Senate votes against someone, the President will have to choose someone else.

When a judge becomes a Supreme Court Justice, he takes an oath promising to do his or her job well and to defend the Constitution.

¿Quién Paga por el Gobierno?

Si te pones a pensar, te darás cuenta que el gobierno te brinda muchos servicios que cuestan dinero. El gobierno financia la educación pública y aporta dinero a muchas universidades. Presta servicios sociales a los pobres y los desventajados. Paga por las carreteras. Se necesita dinero para pagar los sueldos de los funcionarios del gobierno y los gastos de operación.

¿Cómo se paga todo esto? La respuesta es muy sencilla. El pueblo lo paga. Lo paga con sus impuestos.

Hay varios tipos de impuestos. La mayoría de las personas paga impuestos sobre sus ingresos, y muchas también pagan impuestos sobre las ventas de productos tales como cigarrillos, licores, armas de fuego y gasolina. Hay impuestos sobre la finca raíz que se gravan a los propietarios de terrenos y de edificios. Hay impuestos sobre las herencias que se gravan a los herederos. Las compañías también pagan impuestos para sostener al gobierno.

El gobierno mantiene un cuidadoso inventario de sus gastos, puesto que está utilizando el dinero de los contribuyentes.

¿Como Se Crean las Leyes Federales?

Uno de los aspectos más importantes que debes aprender sobre el funcionamiento del gobierno federal es la aprobación de las leyes. Una ley comienza como un proyecto. Se puede elaborar el proyecto de ley en la Cámara o en el Senado (a menos que sea sobre los ingresos del gobierno y en ese caso tiene que comenzar en la Cámara). Elabora y presenta el proyecto un congresista, bien sea senador o representante, pero muchas personas usan su influencia

Who Pays for Government?

If you stop to think for a minute, you will realize that government provides you with many services that cost money. The government pays for public education, and it contributes to some schools of higher education. It provides many social services to poor and handicapped people. It pays for highways. Money is also needed to pay legislators and to run the government. How is all this paid for? The answer is simple. The people pay for the government. They do this when they pay taxes.

There are many different kinds of taxes. Most people pay income taxes, and many people also pay sales tax on certain items such as cigarettes, liquor, firearms, and gasoline. There are also real estate taxes and property taxes for people who own land and buildings. There are inheritance taxes for people who inherit money or property. Businesses also pay taxes to support the government.

The government must keep careful records of the money it spends, since it uses the taxpayers' money.

How Are Laws Made?

One of the most important things you can understand about how government works is the way that laws are passed. A bill, or law, begins as a proposal. It may start in either the House or Senate (unless it is a money bill, when it must start in the House). A bill must be introduced by a legislator, either a representative or a senator, but many people influence legislators to propose a bill. The President may suggest that a bill is needed, or a special or standing

con los congresistas para que se presenten proyectos. El mismo Presidente puede insinuar la necesidad de algún proyecto, o alguna de las comisiones especiales o permanentes del Congreso pueden recomendar algún proyecto. A veces grupos ajenos, con intereses creados, algunos formados por ciudadanos comunes, pueden recomendar algún proyecto a sus congresistas.

Una vez presentado o propuesto un proyecto de ley, se le asigna un número y, aún más importante, se remite a una comisión permanente. Las dos cámaras del Congreso tienen sus comisiones permanentes que estudian los proyectos en sus respectivos campos especiales. Algunas veces, se nombran comisiones especiales. Por ejemplo, un proyecto sobre impuestos se remitiría a la comisión financiera. Un proyecto sobre la salud se remitiría a la comisión de salud. La comisión estudia cuidadosamente el proyecto antes de determinar qué actitud tomar referente al proyecto. Puede archivarlo, o sea no hacer nada. Puede cambiar el proyecto o redactarlo de nuevo. Luego recomienda aprobación o desaprobación a la cámara a la cual pertenece. Si un representante presenta un proyecto, se remite a una comisión de la Cámara. Si un senador presenta un proyecto, se remite a una comisión del Senado.

Terminado el estudio de la comisión y hecha su recomendación, el proyecto pasa a la consideración de la cámara correspondiente para el voto de los congresistas. Si lo aprueban pasa luego a la consideración de la otra cámara. En cualquiera de las dos cámaras se puede desaprobar un proyecto.

Una vez aprobado por las dos cámaras del Congreso, el proyecto pasa al Presidente para su firma o su veto. El Presidente tiene diez días de plazo para tomar alguna acción. Si en esos diez días el Congreso termina su sesión y el Presidente no firma el proyecto, es un "veto de bolsillo."

committee of either house may suggest a bill. Sometimes outside interest groups, often formed of regular citizens, may suggest a bill to their legislators.

Once a bill has been proposed, it is assigned a number and, more important, a committee. Both houses have regular, or standing, committees that study bills in special areas. Sometimes special committees are set up. A bill about taxes would go to a finance committee, for example. A bill about health would go to a committee on health. The committee studies the bill carefully before deciding what action to take. They can do several things with a bill. They can "pigeonhole" it, which means that it will stay in committee—basically nothing will happen to it. They can change or rewrite a bill. After that, they usually pass on it, and recommend to the House or Senate whether they think the law should be passed. If a bill starts in the Senate, it will go to a Senate committee. If it starts in the House of Representatives, it will go to one of the Houses's committees.

When the committee has finished its work, the bill goes to the floor of the House or Senate so all the members can vote on it. When it is done in one house it goes to the other house for approval or disapproval. The members of either house can stop a bill.

After both houses have passed a bill, it goes to the President, so he can sign it or veto it. Sometimes he can veto a bill simply by failing to sign it within ten days after Congress presents it to him. This is called a "pocket veto."

Algunas veces, el Congreso se decide a anular el veto presidencial. Con un nuevo voto, esta vez con mayoría de dos tercios en ambas cámaras, el proyecto entra en vigencia como ley a pesar del veto.

Si alguna vez te encuentras en Washington, D.C., podrás ir al Capitolio para observar la creación de las leyes en el Senado y en la Cámara de Representantes.

Sometimes, Congress will decide to kill a presidential veto. To do this, both houses of Congress must overrule the President with a two-thirds majority vote.

If you are ever in Washington, D.C., you may want to visit either the Senate or the House of Representatives to see for yourself how bills get passed.

4
Los Gobiernos Estatales

¿Qué Es el Gobierno Estatal?

Ya te habrás dado cuenta que los estados son una parte integral de nuestro sistema político debido a que la Constitución de los Estados Unidos deja muchas responsabilidades en manos de ellos.

Los gobiernos estatales se basan en constituciones estatales. En los estados también se divide el gobierno en tres ramas al igual que el gobierno federal. Hay una rama legislativa para crear las leyes estatales; hay una rama ejecutiva que, en el caso de los estados, es encabezado por el Gobernador; hay un sistema judicial de cortes estatales.

Muchas de las constituciones estatales son más complicadas que la Constitución federal. Detallan los derechos de los ciudadanos del estado. Reglamentan la fundación de municipios en el territorio del estado y, frecuentemente, detallan las clases de propiedad exenta de impuestos estatales.

Los gobiernos estatales tienen responsabilidades que se relacionan con muchos aspectos de la vida diaria como son

4

State Governments

What Is State Government?

As you have probably realized, states are a very important part of our government since the United States Constitution leaves so many areas of responsibility to them.

State constitutions are the basis for state governments. State constitutions are the supreme law of states. Most state constitutions divide the governments into three branches just like the federal government. There is a legislative, or lawmaking branch; an executive branch, which is often the governor's office; and a judicial system of state courts.

State constitutions are often much more complicated than federal ones. Many list the rights of the citizens of the state. They often tell how the communities within the states are to be set up. They also often list the kinds of property that the state cannot tax.

States regulate many areas of people's lives, such as banking, health, protection of property and lives, education, taxation, protection of industry and natural resources, and agriculture. In addition to running the public schools,

la banca, la salud, la protección de la propiedad y la vida, la educación, los impuestos, la protección de la industria y los recursos naturales, y la agricultura. Además de dirigir y financiar la educación escolar pública, mantiene universidades y otros centros educativos, tales como los programas de educación para adultos.

¿Cómo Funciona la Rama Ejecutiva Estatal?

Elegido por los votantes de su estado, un gobernador ejerce el poder ejecutivo en un estado. Las responsabilidades de un gobernador varían de un estado a otro pero son muy semejantes. Las funciones típicas de un gobernador son:

1. Supervisar los departamentos y agencias gubernamentales del estado.
2. Nombrar a los funcionarios estatales y despedir a los que no desempeñan bien sus funciones.
3. Ordenar la intervención de la milicia estatal o la policía en tiempo de emergencia o desórdenes, para proteger la propiedad y los ciudadanos.
4. Preparar el presupuesto estatal.
5. Recomendar leyes a la rama legislativa. (La mayoría de los gobernadores tienen el poder del veto.)
6. Mantener comunicación con los funcionarios del gobierno federal en Washington, D.C., responsables por los fondos federales destinados a los estados.
7. Indultar a las personas sentenciadas en las cortes estatales.

Al no poder desempeñar sus funciones, un gobernador queda reemplazado por el vice-gobernador u otro funcionario estatal de alto rango según estipula la constitución estatal. Los gobernadores tienen también funcionarios y administradores que les ayudan a manejar el gobierno

many states also support universities and colleges, and they may run adult education programs.

How Does the Executive Branch of State Government Work?

A governor is the chief executive of a state. The duties of a governor vary slightly from state to state, but here is a list of the typical responsibilities of a state governor:

1. Supervising state departments and agencies.
2. Appointing people to office and removing people who do not work well.
3. Ordering the state militia or police to act to protect people or property in times of emergency or civil disorder.
4. Preparing the state budget.
5. Recommending bills to the legislature. (Most governors also can veto bills.)
6. Maintaining contact with officials in Washington, D.C., who are responsible for supplying federal funds to the states.
7. Pardoning someone who has committed a serious crime.

When a governor cannot perform his duties, he is often replaced by a lieutenant governor or some other top official. Governors also have state officials and administrators to help them run state governments, just as the President has the Cabinet and departments.

estatal al igual que el Presidente tiene su Gabinete y los departamentos.

Aunque hasta ahora ninguna mujer ha sido elegida Presidente de los Estados Unidos, varias han ocupado la gobernación estatal, elegidas por los votantes.

¿Cómo Funciona la Rama Legislativa Estatal?

El poder legislativo lo ejerce una legislatura en los estados. En algunos estados la llaman "Asamblea General," en otros "Asamblea Legislativa," pero en la mayoría "legislatura." Las responsabilidades son las mismas llámese como se llame.

En todos los estados, menos Nebraska, la legislatura está dividida en dos cámaras como el Congreso Nacional. El número de representantes en la legislatura varía de estado a estado.

La cámara alta generalmente es llamada el Senado, y la cámara baja, la Cámara de Representantes o Asamblea. Los legisladores, así se llaman los diputados de la legislatura cuando no se quiere distinguir entre las dos cámaras, son electos por términos de dos a cuatro años, generalmente.

La legislatura aprueba los proyectos de ley de la misma manera que el Congreso. Un legislador presenta un proyecto, se remite a una comisión y luego lo considera la cámara correspondiente antes de pasarlo a la otra cámara y finalmente al gobernador.

Although a woman has not yet been elected President of the United States, several women have served as state governors.

How Does the Legislative Branch of State Government Work?

The lawmaking body of most states is a legislature. Other names for a state legislature are General Assembly or Legislative Assembly, but they all have the same responsibilities.

In all states except Nebraska, state legislatures are divided into two houses, just as Congress is. The size of the state legislature varies from state to state because some states have more people living in them than others do.

The upper house is usually called the Senate, and the lower house is usually called the House of Representatives or Assembly. The legislators, or elected members of the legislature, usually hold office for two to four years.

State legislatures pass bills the same way that Congress does. Bills are proposed by members, sent to committees, and then voted on by one house before being passed on to the other house.

¿Cómo Funciona el Sistema Judicial Estatal?

Los sistemas judiciales de los estados son muy semejantes al sistema federal. En general, están organizados en tres niveles. En el nivel de tribunales inferiores se ven las causas y pleitos civiles y criminales. Luego existe el nivel de apelación, las cortes que consideran de nuevo ciertos casos. En todos los estados hay una corte que funciona a un nivel más alto como corte suprema aún cuando se llame de otra manera. En muchos estados, a diferencia del sistema federal, los magistrados son elegidos por los votantes; no tienen un nobramiento vitalicio.

How Does the State Judicial System Work?

State judicial systems are very much like the federal judicial system. They are usually organized on three levels. First is the lower court level. This is where civil and criminal cases are tried. Next is the appellate level, where cases heard in the lower courts may be heard again. Then, almost all states have a court that functions as a supreme court, although these courts go by several different names depending on the state.

When Did Your State Enter the Union?

Although you do not need to know the following information for your citizenship test, you may be interested to know when your state entered the Union.

¿Cuándo Entró Tu Estado a la Unión?

No es necesario saber este dato para el examen de naturalización pero tal vez te interesa saber en qué fecha tu estado vino a formar parte de los Estados Unidos.

Alabama	December 14, 1819
Alaska	January 3, 1959
Arizona	February 14, 1912
Arkansas	June 15, 1836
California	September 9, 1850
Colorado	August 1, 1876
Connecticut	January 9, 1788
Delaware	December 7, 1787
Florida	March 3, 1845
Georgia	January 2, 1788
Hawaii	August 21, 1959
Idaho	July 3, 1890
Illinois	December 3, 1818
Indiana	December 11, 1816
Iowa	December 28, 1846
Kansas	January 29, 1861
Kentucky	June 1, 1792
Louisiana	April 30, 1812
Maine	March 15, 1820
Maryland	April 28, 1788
Massachusetts	February 6, 1788
Michigan	January 26, 1837
Minnesota	May 11, 1858

Mississippi	December 10, 1817
Missouri	August 10, 1821
Montana	November 8, 1889
Nebraska	March 1, 1867
Nevada	October 31, 1864
New Hampshire	June 21, 1788
New Jersey	December 18, 1787
New Mexico	January 6, 1912
New York	July 26, 1788
North Carolina	November 21, 1789
North Dakota	November 2, 1889
Ohio	March 1, 1803
Oklahoma	November 16, 1907
Oregon	February 14, 1859
Pennsylvania	December 12, 1787
Rhode Island	May 29, 1790
South Carolina	May 23, 1788
South Dakota	November 2, 1889
Tennessee	June 1, 1796
Texas	December 29, 1845
Utah	January 4, 1896
Vermont	March 4, 1791
Virginia	June 25, 1788
Washington	November 11, 1889
West Virginia	June 20, 1863
Wisconsin	May 29, 1848
Wyoming	July 10, 1890

5
Los Gobiernos Locales

¿Qué Es el Gobierno Local?

Al desembarcar en América los primeros colonos, se organizaron en comunidades para gobernarse. Los gobiernos comunales, o sea gobiernos locales, son la forma gubernamental más antigua de los Estados Unidos. Por consiguiente, los norteamericanos se interesan mucho en su gobierno local. Muchos se sienten más cercanos al gobierno local que al federal o al estatal.

Los estados organizan los gobiernos locales. Puede haber provisiones referentes a ellos en la constitución estatal, y algunos estados expiden estatutos de personería jurídica y razón política a los gobiernos locales. Estos estatutos son documentos oficiales dándole a los gobiernos locales el derecho a existir.

En algunos aspectos los gobiernos locales son como versiones en miniatura de los gobiernos federal y estatal. Frecuentemente tienen un ejecutivo y unos departamentos administrativos encabezados por funcionarios como los Secretarios del Gabinete. También tienen un cuerpo legislativo y pueden recaudar impuestos.

Sin embargo, en un aspecto importante, los gobiernos locales son diferentes a los estatales y al federal. Mientras

5

Local Governments

What Is Local Government?

When the first settlers stepped on American land, they organized communities so they could govern themselves. Community governments—also called local governments—are the oldest form of government in the United States. For this reason, Americans often show a lot of interest in their local government. Many people feel more in touch with their local government than with the federal or state government.

Local governments are organized by the states. They may be mentioned in the state constitution, and some states even give charters to local government. A charter is an official paper giving a local government the right to exist.

In some ways, as you will see, local governments are like the federal government. They often have a chief executive, as well as a lawmaking body similar to Congress. They may have departments that are run by people who are similar to Cabinet Secretaries. They can collect taxes.

In one main way, though, local governments are different from federal and state governments. This is because

los gobiernos estatales y el federal pueden destinar fondos para la operación de las escuelas públicas, por ejemplo, son los gobiernos locales que contratan la construcción de los edificios escolares. Contratan a los profesores. Supervisan la educación de los alumnos de manera muy directa.

Hay distintas clases de gobiernos locales. La mayoría de los estados están divididos en condados y también tienen municipios y poblaciones menores como pueblos y aldeas.

Los condados y los municipios y otras poblaciones organizadas políticamente coordinan sus labores cuidadosamente. Un municipio y el condado circundante pueden recaudar impuestos en conjunto o pueden construir una carretera conjuntamente. Esta colaboración es necesaria para que el pueblo sea bien servido por su gobierno local.

¿Qué Son los Gobiernos de Condado?

Llámese condado o, como en Luisiana, parroquia, todos los estados se han organizado con gobiernos regionales, que aquí llamaremos condados. Mientras los municipios y las aldeas sirven a una comunidad de vecinos cercanos, un condado puede incluir varios municipios y aldeas además de los terrenos agrícolas que los rodean. Algunas ciudades son tan grandes que el municipio ocupa casi todo un condado. Chicago, por ejemplo, es un municipio y cubre la totalidad del Condado de Cook.

Los gobiernos de los condados colaboran estrechamente con los gobiernos locales para prestar los servicios obligatorios al pueblo. Además, la mayoría de los condados brindan ciertos servicios independientemente. Un condado tendrá su propia policía encabezada por un alguacil. Unos condados son responsables por las escuelas públicas de la región, y también por la construcción y el mantenimiento de carreteras y caminos cercanos. Prestan servicios de acueductos y

130

local governments provide services directly to people. Where federal or state governments may provide money to run schools, for example, local governments often hire the people to build the schools. They hire the teachers. They supervise the education of children in a direct way.

There are many different kinds of local governments. Most states are divided into counties, and most states also have towns and cities, townships, or villages.

Counties and cities or towns (or whatever the local form of government is called where you live) often coordinate their work carefully. A city and county may collect taxes together, or they may work together to build a highway. This cooperation is important if people are to receive all the services they need from their local governments.

What Are County Governments?

Although counties may go by other names (some are called parishes, for example), all states are organized into some form of county government. While cities and towns often serve a community of people who live close together, a county often includes several cities and towns as well as the farms that surround them. Some cities, though, are so large that they take up most of a county. Chicago, for example, is both a city and a county (Cook County).

County governments mostly work closely with local governments to provide services to people. In addition, most counties provide some independent services. A county may have its own police force, often headed by a sheriff. Some counties are responsible for school systems. Counties are often responsible for maintaining and building highways and roads. They may provide water and sewage

alcantarillado en las comarcas rurales que no forman parte de un municipio o aldea. La mayoría de los condados también tienen un sistema tribunal.

Un servicio prestado frecuentemente por los condados es el registro y archivo de documentos importantes. Un departamento del condado es responsable de registrar los nacimientos, casamientos, muertes, y documentos como títulos de bienes raíces e hipotecas.

Generalmente, los gobiernos de los condados son dirigidos por funcionarios elegidos. Estos encabezan sus respectivos departamentos. Algunos de estos funcionarios son responsables de lo siguiente:

> Registro del Condado—registra y archiva los documentos importantes.
> Tesorero—supervisa las cuentas y paga lo autorizado; mantiene los libros de contabilidad.
> Contralor o Interventor—examina los libros para asegurar que se gasta el dinero según es autorizado.
> Ingeniero—planifica y lleva a cabo la construcción de carreteras y edificios que corresponde al condado.
> Alguacil—dirige la policía del condado.
> Fiscal—procesa los casos criminales que son la responsabilidad del condado.
> Superintendente de escuelas—dirige los servicios y programas educativos.

Como verás cuando leas acerca de los gobiernos locales, las ciudades y los pueblos emplean, en gran parte, el mismo plan de organización.

¿Cómo Está Organizado el Gobierno Local?

Los condados son gobiernos locales, pero, en general, cuando hablamos del gobierno local nos referimos al municipio donde vivimos, bien sea una ciudad grande o una pequeña aldea. Los gobiernos municipales generalmente

services to rural areas that are not part of towns and cities. Most counties also have a court system.

One service that is often provided by counties is the keeping of important records. An entire county department may be responsible for recording births, marriages, and deaths and for property records such as deeds and mortgages.

County governments are usually run by elected officials. Each official usually runs a department in the county. Some of the officials and their department responsibilities are:

> County clerk or recorder—Responsible for keeping important records
>
> Treasurer—Controls the money and pays bills when asked to do so by department heads; keeps written records of how money is spent
>
> County auditor—Examines the financial records to be sure that money is spent the way it is supposed to be
>
> County engineer—Plans and carries out the building of county roads and any buildings for which the county is responsible
>
> Sheriff—Provides police protection
>
> County attorney—Prosecutes criminal cases that are the responsibility of the county
>
> Superintendent of schools—Runs the county's educational program and services

As you will see when you read about city or local governments, many of these same departments are also used by cities and towns to organize the services they provide.

How Is Local Government Organized?

Counties are local governments, but when most people speak about their local government, they usually mean the city, town, or village where they live. In some ways, local governments are like the federal government. They often

133

tienen un ejecutivo llamado el alcalde. Tienen un concejo municipal o asamblea para crear leyes locales que funciona como el Congreso pero suele tener una sola cámara. Como los gobiernos estatales y federales, los gobiernos municipales gravan impuestos para pagar los gastos de los servicios prestados.

A diferencia del gobierno federal y aun de algunos estatales, los gobiernos municipales prestan sus servicios y su protección directamente al pueblo. Aunque utilicen fondos federales o estatales para sufragar sus gastos, los gobiernos municipales se responsabilizan por los siguientes servicios: acueductos y alcantarillados; recolección de basura; educación pública; mantenimiento de calles, edificios públicos y parques; regulación del tránsito; alumbrado en las vías públicas; y protección de la propiedad y la vida a través de la policía y los bomberos. Los municipios suelen tener tribunales también. El sistema judicial local, que puede ser un sólo juez en el caso de una aldea, procesa las causas civiles y criminales menores que ocurran en el municipio.

Funcionarios elegidos dirigen los gobiernos de la mayoría de los municipios. Supervisan los servicios y gravan impuestos para pagar los gastos. Los gobiernos municipales se pueden organizar de varias maneras. Una de éstas es el plan de alcalde y concejo. Los votantes eligen un alcalde y los concejales. Los concejales pueden elegirse por distritos o por el municipio entero. El alcalde gobierna el municipio y lo hace con la ayuda de los departamentos especiales tales como el departamento de bomberos o el departamento de vías y alumbrados públicos. El concejo municipal crea las leyes locales.

El segundo tipo de organización es el plan de administrador y concejo. Es igual al plan de alcalde y concejo pero el

have a chief executive, who is usually called a mayor. They have a lawmaking body such as a city council or assembly, which operates much the same way that Congress does. Like the federal government, local governments can tax their citizens to pay for services, and they spend the tax money to provide services.

Unlike the federal government and even some state governments, local governments are directly involved in providing services and protection to people. Federal and state money may be used to support these services, but it is the local government that actually maintains a police force, collects garbage, supplies water, and runs the schools.

Local government services include such things as supplying water, removing garbage and other sewage, maintaining schools, maintaining local roads and buildings, caring for parks, regulating traffic, and providing street lights, as well as fire and police protection. City and town governments usually have a court system, too. The local court system, which may be only one judge in a small town, handles civil and criminal cases that occur in the community.

Elected officials run most communities. They supervise the services and raise taxes to pay for them.

City governments may be organized in one of several ways. One way is the mayor–city council plan. The people elect a mayor and representatives to the city council. Usually, everyone votes for the mayor, and people choose representatives to the city council from their own districts. Sometimes, though, everyone elects all the representatives or council members. The mayor is responsible for running the city, and he does this with the help of special departments such as the fire department or the streets and lights department. The city council is responsible for making laws.

ejecutivo no es un alcalde elegido sino un administrador, o sea un gerente o director profesional contratado por el concejo. Además de crear leyes, bajo este plan el concejo ejerce también el poder ejecutivo supremo porque el administrador es su empleado.

El tercer tipo de gobierno municipal es el plan de comisarios. Un pequeño grupo de comisarios gobierna el municipio. Son elegidos por los votantes y cada uno es responsable por un departamento.

Hay una forma más de gobierno municipal que todavía se encuentra en los estados de la región llamada Nueva Inglaterra. Es la reunión comunal o vecinal. Las reuniones comunales fueron la primera forma de gobierno local en las colonias, así que es un sistema antiguo. Una población gobernada por una reunión comunal cubre de veinticinco a cuarenta millas cuadradas. Incluye a los agricultores que viven en el campo además de los que viven en la misma comunidad. Una vez al año se efectúa una reunión vecinal para decidir un plan de acción comunal para el año venidero. Hay dos clases de reuniones comunales. En algunos municipios todos los votantes asisten a la reunión y todos pueden opinar. En los municipios más grandes los votantes eligen representantes para que asistan a la reunión. Durante el año, los servicios diarios están administrados por funcionarios elegidos. Frecuentemente, una junta o un concejo crea leyes y las hace cumplir. Un registrador registra los documentos públicos, y una junta educacional y un superintendente dirigen las escuelas. Aunque la mayoría de los municipios tienen el plan de alcalde y concejo, es interesante saber algo sobre las reuniones comunales porque representan un ejemplo importante de la participación directa del pueblo en su gobierno.

Para averiguar quiénes son los funcionarios gubernamentales del municipio y del estado donde vives, o quiénes son tus representantes en Washington, D.C., llama por teléfono a la biblioteca pública o a la alcaldía local.

The second form of local government is the city manager–council plan. This is like the mayor–city council plan, except the chief executive is hired, rather than elected. A city manager is responsible to city council members. They run the city, in addition to passing laws.

The third form of organization is the commissioner plan. A small group of officials called commissioners run the local government. They are usually elected by the citizens. Each commissioner is usually responsible for one department.

There is one more form of local government, which is still found in the New England states. It is the town meeting. Town meetings were the very first form of local government, so this is an old system. A community governed by a town meeting is usually an area twenty-five to forty square miles. It includes not only those people who live in the town but also the farmers who live outside the town or village. Once every year, a town meeting is held to decide what will be done in the community during the coming year. There are two kinds of town meetings. In some towns, everyone attends the town meeting, and everyone has a say in the local government, and in other, larger towns, people elect representatives to attend the town meetings for them. Between town meetings, the day-to-day services are supervised by elected officials. An elected board or council often makes and enforces laws. A clerk keeps records, and a school board, headed by a superintendent, runs the schools. Although most local governments are run by a mayor and city council, town meetings are still interesting to know about because they are an important example of how people participate directly in government.

To find out who your mayor, governor, lieutenant governor, and senators are, call your local library or City Hall.

Part Three

SAMPLE
QUESTIONS
AND ANSWERS

Tercera Parte

PREGUNTAS (Q)
Y RESPUESTAS (A)

1.Q. **In what country do you live?**
   A. I live in the United States of America.

2.Q. **How many states are in the United States?**
   A. There are fifty states.

3.Q. **What is the capital of your state?**
   A. The capitals are listed on page 46-47.

4.Q. **Who discovered America?**
   A. Christopher Columbus discovered America.

5.Q. **How many original states did America have?**
   A. There were thirteen original states.

6.Q. **Why is July 4 an important date in U.S. history?**
   A. America declared independence on that date.

7.Q. **Why was the Revolutionary War fought?**
   A. It was America's fight for independence from Britain.

8.Q. **Who was the first President of the United States?**
   A. George Washington was the first President.

9.Q. **What was the Louisiana Purchase?**
   A. It was the largest single chunk of land added to the United States at one time. It was bought from France.

10.Q. **What is the Monroe Doctrine?**
   A. In 1823, President Monroe announced that the United States would protect all American countries from European interference. The Monroe Doctrine also stated that no foreign powers would be allowed to start colonies in the Americas.

11.Q. **What was the Civil War?**
 A. It was a war between the North and the South. The war was fought over the issue of slavery.

12.Q. **Is Puerto Rico a state?**
 A. No, it is a commonwealth of the United States.

13.Q. **What is the Constitution of the United States?**
 A. It is a written document that contains many laws and says how the federal government should be organized. It explains and limits the powers of the federal government. It is the highest law of the land.

14.Q. **How many parts does the Constitution have?**
 A. The Constitution has three parts. The first part is the Preamble. The main body has seven articles. Then there are twenty-six amendments.

15.Q. **How can the Constitution be amended?**
 A. Two thirds of both houses of Congress have to vote for an amendment or a national convention may be requested by two thirds of the States. At the convention, two thirds of the states must support the amendment. Then, a majority vote in three fourths of the states or in three fourths of state conventions held for this purpose must be obtained.

16.Q. **What is the Bill of Rights?**
 A. The Bill of Rights is the first ten amendments to the Constitution. It guarantees individual citizens' rights.

17.Q. **What is the Preamble to the Constitution?**
 A. It is the introduction. It explains why we need a Constitution.

18.Q. **What is the basis of local government?**

A. Most local governments exist because the state constitutions say they should exist. Some state constitutions provide charters to local governments.

19.Q. **How do governments pay for the services they provide to people?**

A. They raise and collect taxes from people to pay for the services.

20.Q. **What is a city council?**

A. A city council is the legislative branch of local government. It is made up of elected representatives, who are responsible for passing laws and sometimes also for running the city departments.

21.Q. **What are some important services provided by local governments?**

A. Local governments provide fire and police protection, run schools, maintain streets and parks, and keep important records, among other things.

22.Q. **What is a county?**

A. A county is a form of local government that often includes several towns and cities and the surrounding farms.

23.Q. **How does a county government work?**

A. A county is run by a board of officials who are elected by the people.

24.Q. **Who are some county officers?**

A. Some county officers are sheriff, county clerk, treasurer, auditor, county engineer, county attorney, and superintendent of schools.

25. Q. **What is a state Constitution?**
   A. The state Constitution is the basic law of the state. It is the basis of the state government.

26. Q. **Who are the governor and lieutenant governor of your state?**
   A. (Answers will vary.)

27. Q. **What are a governor's responsibilities?**
   A. The governor's main responsibilities are to carry out the laws passed by the state legislature and to supervise the state departments and agencies.

28. Q. **Who makes the laws for the state?**
   A. The laws are passed by state legislatures.

29. Q. **How many houses are in state legislatures?**
   A. All states except Nebraska have two houses. The upper house is usually called the Senate, and the lower house is called the House of Representatives.

30. Q. **What is the term of state legislators?**
   A. They are elected either for two- or four-year terms, depending on the state.

31. Q. **What cases are tried in federal courts?**
   A. The cases tried are about federal laws, suits between states, cases involving foreign diplomats, and those involving an American citizen and a foreign country.

32. Q. **What is the capital of the United States?**
   A. The capital of the United States is Washington, D.C.

33.Q. What form of government does the United States have?

 A. The government of the United States is a republic. A republic is government by the people through representatives elected by the people. Because the people are free, the United States is also a democracy.

34.Q. What are the three branches of federal government?

 A. The three branches of federal government are the executive (the President), the legislative (the Congress), and the judicial (the Supreme Court) branches.

35.Q. Who is the chief executive of the United States?

 A. The chief executive of the United States is the President.

36.Q. What are the President's chief powers and duties?

 A. The chief powers and duties of the President are to enforce federal laws, advise Congress, make treaties, appoint federal officers, and head the armed forces.

37.Q. How often do we vote for President?

 A. We vote for a President every four years, on the first Tuesday after the first Monday in November.

38.Q. Who can be President?

 A. A citizen born in the United States, at least thirty-five years old, who has lived in the United States for fourteen years can be President.

39.Q. When does the President take office?

 A. He is inaugurated at noon on January 20, following the election in November.

40. Q. In case of death or illness, who fills the office of the President?
   A. The Vice-President would replace the President.

41. Q. What are the chief duties of the Vice-President?
   A. He presides over the Senate and represents the President at many functions.

42. Q. What is the President's Cabinet?
   A. His cabinet are department heads called Secretaries, who advise the President and assist him in his work.

43. Q. What is the legislative branch of federal government?
   A. The legislative branch is Congress.

44. Q. What are the chief duties of Congress?
   A. The chief duties of Congress are to pass federal laws, approve Presidential appointments, approve treaties, and decide how tax money will be spent.

45. Q. How many houses are in Congress?
   A. Congress has two Houses, the Senate and the House of Representatives.

46. Q. How many senators are elected from each state?
   A. There are two senators from each state.

47. Q. Who are the senators from your state?
   A. (Answers will vary.)

48. Q. How many representatives does each state have in Congress?
   A. The number of representatives is based on the population of the state.

49.Q. **How are the representatives and senators elected?**
A. They are elected by the people in the states. Representatives are elected for two years, and senators are elected for six years.

50.Q. **Who presides over the House of Representatives and the Senate?**
A. The Speaker of the House presides over the House of Representatives. The Vice-President officially presides over the Senate, but most of the time, the president *pro tempore* runs the Senate.

51.Q. **What is the highest court in the United States?**
A. The highest court is the United States Supreme Court.

52.Q. **How many judges sit on the United States Supreme Court?**
A. There are nine. One is the Chief Justice, and the other eight are Associate Justices.

53.Q. **What is the term of office for a federal judge?**
A. They hold office for life.

54.Q. **How does the Supreme Court work?**
A. The Supreme Court meets and decides on cases handed in by lower courts. Sometimes, cases go to the Supreme Court directly.

55.Q. **What lower federal courts do we have?**
A. There are one hundred Federal District Courts and ten Federal Circuit Courts of Appeal.

Reprinted by permission from International Institute of Detroit.

APPENDIX
APENDICE

Form I-130
Formulario I-130

U.S. Department of Justice
Immigration and Naturalization Service

OMB No. 1115-0054
Approval expires 4-83

PETITION TO CLASSIFY STATUS OF ALIEN RELATIVE FOR ISSUANCE OF IMMIGRANT VISA

Fee Stamp

(PLEASE NOTE – YOU ARE THE PETITIONER AND YOUR RELATIVE IS THE BENEFICIARY)

TO THE SECRETARY OF STATE:

REMARKS

The petition was filed on _____

The petition is approved for status under section:

		DATE OF ACTION
□ SPOUSE, 201 (b) CHILD	□ 203 (a) (2)	
□ 201 (b) PARENT	□ 203 (a) (4)	DD
	□ 203 (a) (5)	DISTRICT
□ 203 (a) (1)		

- □ PERSONAL INTERVIEW CONDUCTED
- □ DOCUMENT CHECK ONLY
- □ FIELD INVESTIGATION COMPLETED
- □ APPROVAL PREVIOUSLY FORWARDED

(PETITIONER IS NOT TO WRITE ABOVE THIS LINE)

1. Name of beneficiary (Last, in CAPS)   (First)   (Middle)

2. **Do Not Write In This Space**

3. Beneficiary's marital status:
   □ Married □ Widowed □ Divorced □ Single

4. Other names used by beneficiary (including maiden name if married)

5. Has this beneficiary ever been in the U.S.?
   □ YES □ NO

6. Country of beneficiary's birth

7. Date of beneficiary's birth (Month, day, year)

8. Are beneficiary and petitioner related by adoption?
   □ YES □ NO

9. Petitioner's name is: (Last, in CAPS)   (First)   (Middle)

10. petitioner's phone No.

11. The beneficiary is my: (relationship)

12. Other names used by petitioner (including maiden name if married woman)

13. Name of beneficiary's spouse, if married, and date and country of birth (Omit this item if petition is for your spouse)

14. Full address of beneficiary's spouse and children, if any (Omit this item if petition is for your spouse)

15. Names, birthdates and countries of birth of beneficiary's children:

16. Check the appropriate box below and furnish the information required for the box checked:

☐ Beneficiary will apply for a visa abroad at the American Consulate in _____
   (CITY IN FOREIGN COUNTRY) (FOREIGN COUNTRY)

☐ Beneficiary is in the United States and will apply for adjustment of status to that of a lawful permanent resident in the office of the Immigration and Naturalization

Service at _____
         (CITY)   (STATE)

If the application for adjustment of status is denied, the beneficiary will apply for a visa abroad at the American Consulate in

_____   _____
(CITY IN FOREIGN COUNTRY)   (FOREIGN COUNTRY)

17. Address in the United States where beneficiary will reside

_____   _____   _____   _____
                   (City)   (Town or city)   (Province or State)

18. Address at which beneficiary is presently residing   (Apt. No.)   (Number and street)   (Town or city)   (Province or State)   (ZIP Code)

19. (a) Beneficiary's address abroad (if any) is: (Number and Street)   (Town or City)   (Province)   (Country)

(b) If the beneficiary's native alphabet is other than Roman letters, write his/her name and address in the native alphabet:
    (Name)   (Number and Street)   (Town or City)   (Province)   (Country)

OVER

FORM I–130
(Rev. 9-1-82) Y

RECEIVED	TRANS. IN	RET'D. TRANS. OUT	COMPLETED

20. If beneficiary is in the United States, give the following information concerning beneficiary:

(a) Last arrived in U.S. as
(Visitor, student, exchange alien, crewman, stowaway, etc.) on
(Month) (Day) (Year)

(b) Date beneficiary's stay expired or will expire as shown on his Form I-94 or I-95.
(Month) (Day) (Year)

(c) Beneficiary's File number if any
• A-

(d) Name and address of beneficiary's present employer

(e) Date beneficiary began this employment

21. I was born.   (Month)   (Day)   (Year)   in: (Town or city)   (State or Province)   (Country)

22. If you are a citizen of the United States, give the following:
Citizenship was acquired: (Check one)

☐ through birth in the U.S.   ☐ through parents   ☐ through naturalization   ☐ through marriage

(1) If acquired through naturalization, give name under which naturalized or name used prior to naturalization, if different from your present name, number of naturalization certificate, and date and place of naturalization:

(2) If known, my former alien registration number was A _____

(3) If acquired through parentage or marriage, have you obtained a certificate of citizenship in your own name?
(a) If so, give number of certificate and date and place of issuance: _____
(b) If not, submit evidence of citizenship in accordance with instruction 3 a (2)

23. If you are a lawful permanent resident alien of the United States, give the following:

a. Alien Registration Number
A-

b. Date, place, and means of admission for lawful permanent residence

24. If this petition is for your spouse or child, give the following: a. Date and place of your present marriage

b. Names of your prior spouses

c. Names of spouse's prior spouses

25. My residence in the United States is: (C/O, if appropriate) _____ (Apt. No.) _____ (Number and Street) _____ (Town or city) _____ (State) _____ (ZIP Code)

26. My address abroad (if any) is: (Number and street) _____ (Town or city) _____ (Province) _____ (Country)

27. Last address at which I and my spouse resided together (Town or city) _____ (State or Province) _____ (Country) _____ (Number and street) _____ (Apt. No.) _____ From (Month) (Year) _____ To (Month) (Year)

28. If this petition is for a child, (a). is the child married? _____ (b). is the child your adopted child? _____ If so, give the names, dates, and places of birth of all other children adopted by you. If none, so state.

29. If this petition is for a brother or sister, are both your parents the same as the alien's parents? _____ If not, submit a separate statement giving full details as to parentage, dates of marriage of parents, and the number of previous marriages of each parent.

30. If separate petitions are also being submitted for other relatives, give names of each and relationship to petitioner.

31. Have you ever filed a petition for this alien before? _____ If so, give place and date of filing and result.

32.

CERTIFICATION OF PETITIONER

I certify, under penalty of perjury under the laws of the United States of America that the foregoing is true and correct.

Executed on (date) _____ Signature _____

33.

SIGNATURE OF PERSON PREPARING FORM IF OTHER THAN PETITIONER

I declare that this document was prepared by me at the request of the petitioner and is based on all information of which I have any knowledge.

_____ (SIGNATURE) _____ (ADDRESS) _____ (DATE)

Form N-400
Formulario N-400

UNITED STATES DEPARTMENT OF JUSTICE
IMMIGRATION AND NATURALIZATION SERVICE

OMB NO. 1115-0009
Approval Expires 1/31/84

FEE STAMP

APPLICATION TO FILE PETITION FOR NATURALIZATION

Mail or take to:

IMMIGRATION AND NATURALIZATION SERVICE

(See INSTRUCTIONS. BE SURE YOU UNDERSTAND EACH
QUESTION BEFORE YOU ANSWER IT. PLEASE PRINT OR
TYPE.)

ALIEN REGISTRATION

(Show the exact spelling of your name as it appears on your alien registration
receipt card, and the number of your card. If you did not register, so state.)

Name ....

No. ....

Date: ....

Section of Law ....
(Leave Blank)

(1) My full true and correct name is ....
(Full true name without abbreviations)

(2) I now live at ....
(Number and street,)
....
(City, county, state, zip code)

(3) I was born on .... in ....
(Month) (Day) (Year)   (City or town)   (County, province, or state)   (Country)

(4) I request that my name be changed to ....

(5) Other names I have used are: ....
(Include maiden name)   Sex: ☐ Male ☐ Female

(6) Was your father or mother ever a United States citizen? .... ☐ Yes ☐ No
(If "Yes", explain fully)

(7) Can you read and write English? .... ☐ Yes ☐ No

(8) Can you speak English? .... ☐ Yes ☐ No

(9) Can you sign your name in English? .... ☐ Yes ☐ No

(10) My lawful admission for permanent residence was on .... under the name of

....

at ....
(Month)   (Day)   (Year)
   ....
   (City)   (State)

(11) (a) I have resided continuously in the United States since ....
(Month)   (Day)   (Year)

(b) I have resided continuously in the State of .... since ....
(Month)   (Day)   (Year)

(c) During the last five years I have been physically in the United States for a total of .... months.

From	To	Street Address	City and State
(a) ......, 19....	PRESENT TIME		
(b) ......, 19....	......, 19....		
(c) ......, 19....	......, 19....		
(d) ......, 19....	......, 19....		

(14) (a) Have you been out of the United States since your lawful admission as a permanent resident? .... ☐ Yes ☐ No

If "Yes" fill in the following information for every absence of *less than 6 months*, no matter how short it was.

Date Departed	Date Returned	Name of Ship, or of Airline, Railroad Company, Bus Company, or Other Means Used to Return to the United States	Place or Port of Entry Through Which You Returned to the United States

(b) Since your lawful admission, have you been out of the United States for a period of *6 months or longer?* .... ☐ Yes ☐ No

If "No", state "None"; If "Yes", fill in following information for every absence of more than 6 months.

Date Departed	Date Returned	Name of Ship or of Airline, Railroad Company, Bus Company, or Other Means Used to Return to the United States	Place or Port of Entry Through Which You Returned to the United States

(OVER)

Form N-400 (Rev. 4-14-81)Y

(1)

(2)

(15) The law provides that you may not be regarded as qualified for naturalization, if you knowingly committed certain offenses or crimes, even though you may not have been arrested. Have you ever, in or outside the United States:

(a) knowingly committed any crime for which you have not been arrested? .... ☐ Yes ☐ No

(b) been arrested, cited, charged, indicted, convicted, fined or imprisoned for breaking or violating any law or ordinance, including traffic regulations? .... ☐ Yes ☐ No

If you answer "Yes" to (a) or (b), give the following information as to each incident.

WHEN	WHERE (City) (State) (Country)	NATURE OF OFFENSE	OUTCOME OF CASE, IF ANY
(a)			
(b)			
(c)			
(d)			
(e)			

(16) List your present and past membership in or affiliation with every organization, association, fund, foundation, party, club, society or similar group in the United States or in any other country or place, and your foreign military service. (If none, write "None.")

(a) ...., 19...... to 19......
(b) ...., 19...... to 19......
(c) ...., 19...... to 19......
(d) ...., 19...... to 19......
(e) ...., 19...... to 19......
(f) ...., 19...... to 19......
(g) ...., 19...... to 19......

(17) (a) Are you now, or have you ever, in the United States or in any other place, been a member of, or in any other way connected or associated with the Communist Party? (If "Yes", attach full explanation) .... ☐ Yes ☐ No

(b) Have you ever knowingly aided or supported the Communist Party directly, or indirectly through another organization, group or person? (If "Yes", attach full explanation) .... ☐ Yes ☐ No

(c) Do you now or have you ever advocated, taught, believed in, or knowingly supported or furthered the interests of Communism? (If "Yes", attach full explanation) .... ☐ Yes ☐ No

(18) During the period March 23, 1933 to May 8, 1945, did you serve in, or were you in any affiliated with, either directly or indirectly, any military unit, paramilitary unit, police unit, self-defense unit, vigilante unit, citizen unit, unit of the Nazi Party or SS, government agency or office, extermination camp, concentration camp, prisoner of war camp, prison, labor camp, detention camp or transit camp, under the control of or affiliated with:

(a) the Nazi Government of Germany .... ☐ Yes ☐ No
(b) any Government in any area occupied by, allied with, or established with the assistance or cooperation of, the Nazi Government of Germany? .... ☐ Yes ☐ No

(19) During the period March 23, 1933 to May 8, 1945, did you ever order, incite, assist, or otherwise participate in the persecution of any person because of race, religion, national origin, or political opinion? .... ☐ Yes ☐ No

(20) Have you borne any hereditary title or have you been of any order of nobility in any foreign state? .... ☐ Yes ☐ No

(21) **Have you ever been declared legally incompetent or have you ever been confined as a patient in a mental institution?** .... ☐ Yes ☐ No

(22) Are deportation proceedings pending against you, or have you ever been deported or ordered deported, or have you ever applied for suspension of deportation? .... ☐ Yes ☐ No

(23) (a) My last Federal income tax return was filed.............. (year)   Do you owe any Federal taxes? .... ☐ Yes ☐ No
(b) Since becoming a permanent resident of the United States, have you:
—filed an income tax return as a nonresident? .... ☐ Yes ☐ No
—failed to file an income tax return because you regarded yourself as a nonresident? .... ☐ Yes ☐ No
(If you answer "Yes" to (a) or (b) explain fully.)

(24) Have you ever claimed in writing, or in any other way, to be a United States citizen? .... ☐ Yes ☐ No

(25) (a) Have you ever deserted from the military, air, or naval forces of the United States? .... ☐ Yes ☐ No
(b) If male, have you ever left the United States to avoid being drafted into the Armed Forces of the United States? .... ☐ Yes ☐ No

(26) The law provides that you may not be regarded as qualified for naturalization if, at *any* time during the period for which you are required to prove good moral character, you have been a habitual drunkard; committed adultery; advocated or practiced polygamy; have been a prostitute or procured anyone for prostitution; have knowingly and for gain helped any alien to enter the United States illegally; have been an illicit trafficker in narcotic drugs or marijuana; have received your income mostly from illegal gambling, or have given false testimony for the purpose of obtaining any benefits under this Act. Have you ever, *anywhere*, been such a person or committed any of these acts?   (If you answer yes to any of these, attach full explanation.) .... ☐ Yes ☐ No

(27) Do you believe in the Constitution and form of government of the United States? .... ☐ Yes ☐ No

(28) Are you willing to take the full oath of allegiance to the United States? (See Instructions) .... ☐ Yes ☐ No

(29) If the law requires it, are you willing:
(a) to bear arms on behalf of the United States? (If "No", attach full explanation) .... ☐ Yes ☐ No
(b) to perform noncombatant services in the Armed Forces of the United States? (If "No", attach full explanation) .... ☐ Yes ☐ No
(c) to perform work of national importance under civilian direction? (If "No", attach full explanation) .... ☐ Yes ☐ No

(30) (a) If male, did you ever register under United States Selective Service laws or draft laws? .... ☐ Yes ☐ No
If "Yes" give date............; Selective Service No............; Local Board No............; Present classification..........
(b) Did you ever apply for exemption from military service because of alienage, conscientious objections, or other reasons? ☐ Yes ☐ No
If "Yes," explain fully..........

(31) If serving or ever served in the Armed Forces of the United States, give branch................ , 19........ , to .... , 19........

from .... , 19........ to .... , 19........ , and from .... , 19........ , to .... , 19........

☐ inducted or ☐ enlisted at .... ; Service No. ....

type of discharge .... (Honorable. Dishonorable. etc.) .... ; rank at discharge ....

reason for discharge ....

(alienage, conscientious objector, other)

☐ Reserve or ☐ National Guard from .... 19........ to ....

(32) My occupation is ....

List the names, addresses, and occupations (or types of business) of your employers during the last 5 years.   (If none, write "None.")

List present employment FIRST.

FROM.	TO.	EMPLOYER'S NAME	ADDRESS	OCCUPATION OR TYPE OF BUSINESS
	PRESENT TIME			
(a) .... , 19	.... , 19			
(b) .... , 19	.... , 19			
(c) .... , 19	.... , 19			
(d) .... , 19	.... , 19			

(33) Complete this block if you are or have been married.

I am .... The first name of my husband or wife is (was) ....
(Separated, married, divorced, widowed)

We were married on .... at .... He or she was born at ....

.... on (date) .... He or she entered the United States at (place) ....

☐ apart from me at .... for permanent residence and now resides ☐ with me
(Show full address if not living with you.)

.... at .... ; Certificate No. ....

He or she was naturalized on .... His or her Alien Registration No. is ....

or became a citizen by ....

(34) How many times have you been married? .... How many times has your husband or wife been married? .... If either of you has been married more than once, fill in the following information for each previous marriage.

DATE MARRIED	DATE MARRIAGE ENDED	NAME OF PERSON TO WHOM MARRIED	SEX	(Check One) PERSON MARRIED WAS CITIZEN / ALIEN	HOW MARRIAGE ENDED
(a)				☐ / ☐	
(b)				☐ / ☐	
(c)				☐ / ☐	
(d)				☐ / ☐	

(35) I have............children: (Complete columns (a) to (h) as to each child. If child lives with you, state "with me" in column (h), otherwise give city and State of child's residence.)
(Number)

(a) Given Names	(b) Sex	(c) Place Born (Country)	(d) Date Born	(e) Date of Entry	(f) Port of Entry	(g) Alien Registration No.	(h) Now Living at -

(36) **READ INSTRUCTION NO. 6 BEFORE ANSWERING QUESTION (36)**

I............want certificates of citizenship for those of my children who are in the U.S. and are under age 18 years that are named below.
(Do)   (Do Not)

(Enclose $15 for each child for whom you want certificates, otherwise, send no money with this application.)

(Write names of children under age 18 years and who are in the U.S. for whom you want certificates)

If present spouse is not the parent of the children named above, give parent's name, date and place of naturalization, and number of marriages.

(4)

Signature of person preparing form, if other than applicant.

I declare that this document was prepared by me at the request of applicant and is based on all information of which I have any knowledge.

SIGNATURE

ADDRESS:

SIGNATURE OF APPLICANT

ADDRESS AT WHICH APPLICANT RECEIVES MAIL

DATE:

APPLICANT'S TELEPHONE NUMBER

TO APPLICANT: DO NOT FILL IN BLANKS BELOW THIS LINE.

NOTE CAREFULLY.—This application must be sworn to before an officer of the Immigration and Naturalization Service at the time you appear before such officer for examination on this application.

AFFIDAVIT

I do swear that I know the contents of this application comprising pages 1 to 4, inclusive, and the supplemental forms thereto, No(s). _____, subscribed to by me; that the same are true to the best of my knowledge and belief; that corrections numbered ( ) to ( ) were made by me or at my request; and that this application was signed by me with my full, true, and correct name, SO HELP ME GOD.

_____
(Complete and true signature of applicant)

_____
(For demonstration of applicant's ability to write English)

Subscribed and sworn to before me by applicant at the preliminary investigation ( ) at _____) or _____

this _____ day of _____, 19___.

I certify that before verification the above applicant stated in my presence that he/she had (heard) read the foregoing application, corrections therein and supplemental form(s) and understood the contents thereof.

_____
(Naturalization examiner)

Nonfiled _____

_____
(Date, Reasons)

1st witness. Occupation _____
2nd witness. Occupation _____

NOTICE TO APPLICANTS:

Authority for collection of the information requested on this form and those forms mentioned in the instructions thereto is contined in Sections 328, 329, 332, 334, 335 or 341 of the Immigration and Nationality Act of 1952 (8 U.S.C. 1439, 1440, 1443, 1445, 1446 or 1452). Submission of the information is voluntary inasmuch as the immigration and nationality laws of the United States do not require an alien to apply for naturalization. If your Social Security number is omitted from a form, no right, benefit or privilege will be denied for your failure to provide such number. However, as military records are indexed by such numbers, verification of your military service, if required to establish eligibility for naturalization, may prove difficult. The principal purposes for soliciting the information are to enable designated officers of the Immigration and Naturalization Service to determine the admissibility of a petitioner for naturalization and to make appropriate recommendations to the naturalization courts. All or any part of the information solicited may, as a matter of routine use, be disclosed to a court exercising naturalization jurisdiction and to other federal, state, local or foreign law enforcement or regulatory agencies, Department of Defense, including any component thereof, the Selective Service System, the Department of State, the Department of the Treasury, Central Intelligence Agency, Interpol and individuals and organizations in the processing of the application or petition for naturalization, or during the course of investigation to elicit further information required by the Immigration and Naturalization Service to carry out its function. Information solicited which indicates a violation or potential violation of law, whether civil, criminal or regulatory in nature may be referred, as routine use, to the appropriate agency, whether federal, state, local or foreign, charged with the responsibility of investigating, enforcing or prosecuting such violations. Failure to provide any or all of the solicited information may result in an adverse recommendation to the court as to an alien's eligibility for naturalization and denial by the court of a petition for naturalization.

For sale by the Superintendent of Documents, U.S. Government Printing Office
Washington, D.C. 20402 (per 100)

U.S. GOVERNMENT PRINTING OFFICE : 1981 O—351-296